NINETY YEARS
"AT HOME" IN
PHILADELPHIA

by
Mary Wickham Bond

To John Lukacs,
with many Thanks for introducing
me to historic consciousness and the
remembered past, a state of mind which
has considerably brightened the later
years of my long life — from
Mary Wickham Bond

April 24, 1988
Chestnut Hill

Books by the Author
The Tilted Cup
Cherique
Gloom Creek
Device and Desire
The Petrified Gesture
How 007 Got His Name
Far Afield in the Caribbean
To James Bond With Love

To David,
   who has been a steadfast escort, critic, and
   companion throughout the long journey
   into my remembered past.

ACKNOWLEDGEMENTS

I wish to give my special thanks to the Dorrance and Company's staff for their politeness, interest, and knowledge while editing my manuscript; to John Lear, who, with the stroke of his pen, caught the essence of our city's skyline in his perfect sketch for the front jacket cover; to Hank O'Donnell for his congenial and patient xerox operators at his stationery store; and to Nancy Hubby, for her wisdom and encouragement at the right moments.

Contents

Preface

I HAVE WRITTEN this book as I have lived it, totally unaware until the circle was complete that it would make me see myself in an unfamiliar light. I plunged enthusiastically into the project, following the advice that if you must write you should be sure to choose a subject thoroughly familiar to you. That was easy. Didn't I know myself better than anything else in the world? But did I?

I saw myself as a normal person similar to vast numbers of women not only in America but also abroad, living out their lives in comparable backgrounds of privilege, good parents and good health. In my eyes there was nothing extraordinary about this and, weary of violence, assassinations, hatreds and prejudices and the eternal struggle for personal power, I wanted to "spend" my ninety years in sharing what I considered worth remembering. To sum it up, the heart of the matter has been a private search for companionship.

It was therefore somewhat of a shock to discover at the end of the book that it had developed a strong personality of its own which had nothing to do with me, and was squeezing itself into a tiny niche in history because it records a peep into what has been described as "a lost and enchanted world."

M.W.B.

CHAPTER 1

1898–1920

I CAN REMEMBER WHEN, once upon a time, it was the custom of certain Philadelphia ladies to send out "At Home" cards. Whether these bore a Main line, Penllyn, City, or Chestnut Hill address, all were engraved by J.E. Caldwell, jewelers on Chestnut Street. In one corner of the card below the name of the hostess was her address; on the other, for example, were the words "At Home Thursdays in May, after four o'clock."

Sometimes an at home might take place in the fall, but springtime was the best when those who spent the winter in town had moved to their country estates, giving the ladies the chance to show off not only their gardens but also their new summer dresses of organdy, dotted Swiss, or dimity. Popular at that time were little black velvet bows, lacy sleeves, large lacy hats and parasols. Magnificent silver tea services, presumably heirlooms, were proudly set out and maids in black bombazine, white ruffled caps and aprons passed dainty sandwiches and sponge cakes among the company. The amount of gossip exchanged on these strictly female occasions has never been recorded but each "set" took itself seriously. Of course it sometimes happened that a new face was added which might result in a *grande dame* looking the newcomer in the eye and saying, "My dear! How surprising to see you here! I didn't know you were on Nellie's list."

There are many meanings to the words "at home." I pity those who look back on their childhood where "home" stood for something dreary, unfriendly, or a place to get away from. To me, "home" meant an iron gate in a fence with a mass of lilacs on the right and on the left a tangle of wistaria in which I used to snuggle and watch the bees gathering pollen from the dangling lavender blossoms. Home meant the number 322 on the top step to our Moreland Avenue front porch. It meant rushing home from Miss Landstreet's kindergarten across the street and finding Mother seated at one of the French windows in her bedroom,

1

sewing. It meant singing hymns on Sunday evenings with Mother at the upright piano in the parlour. And it meant *The Wizard of Oz, Tanglewood Tales, Alice in Wonderland* and a series of "My Little Cousin" books—*My Little Japanese Cousin*, or Swedish, French, German—which planted in my mind that to them I must be their "Little American Cousin." Later came *Maria Edgeworth, Little Women* and lots of poetry from the Oxford Book of English Verse. Perhaps the best way to define what the word *home* meant to me is to say it was an opening door to life based on an unshakable sense of security.

I was not alone. This was Chestnut Hill just after the turn of the century, a community within the city limits, unselfconscious and stable. In our Wissahickon Heights area of the parish of St. Martin-in-the-Fields—I dare say in practically all of the houses from the railroad track to the Wissahickon Creek—the children felt exactly as I did. The Woodwards; the Henrys; the E.W. Clarks and Houstons; the Lattas; the Ross and Lewis children; the Nathan Taylors' five daughters; the three Newbold girls; the three McCouch boys; Marion and Mildred Crawley; the George Dallases and Ballards; Shepherds and LeRoys—all these names still meant "home" to me. As far as each one of us was individually concerned, we children all looked at life pretty much the same way and did not realize until much later that a few households were not as blissfully complacent and happy as our own. For there's always a bully somewhere in a neighborhood and a tattletale, as well as jealousies at school and in sports.

Neither of my parents were Philadelphians and it seemed as if most of my school friends had grandparents, cousins and aunts nearby. We had to go to Virginia for our Wickham relatives and to South Carolina for the Porcher (pronounced *por-shay*) and to Hollidaysburg, Pennsylvania for our only living grandparent, Grandmother Landis. Hollidaysburg was a beautiful little town in the heart of the Allegheny Mountains, famous for being the point at which the barges on the Pennsylvania canal were dismantled, carried over the mountains and re-assembled on the other side to continue on their way to Pittsburg or Erie. The town was seven miles outside of Altoona where the ironworks of the Pennsylvania Railroad were situated. Railroading in the 1870s was similar to what aviation was in the 1920s and it was here that the railroad company gathered together a group of college graduates and trained them for future officers when needed. The young civil engineers soon discovered a bevy of pretty girls in Hollidaysburg, and that is how my father met my mother, the daughter of Judge Augustus S. Landis. A train left Hollidaysburg every night at ten o'clock for Altoona, and my mother

reported that the engineer blew his whistle ten minutes before leaving—
a signal that resulted in front doors flying open with young men rushing
out and down to the depot to catch the train. If they missed it they
would have to walk the seven miles to Altoona to be on hand for work
the next morning.

Mother had two younger sisters, Aunt Helen Dibert and Aunt Letitia
Shelby, both of whom, like Grandmother, lived in Hollidaysburg. There
were seven of us grandchildren but, because my sister Eleanor and I
were the oldest, we did not see very much of our younger cousins. The
family scattered after we were all married and today only Evelyn Dibert
Hollar and I are the remaining survivors of the seven.

As a child I loved Grandmother's garden with nasturtiums, and
poppies, hollyhocks and zinnias and gravelled paths and garden beds
edged with wooden boards. I also loved to hear her rip up and down
her large box piano, diamonds and rubies flashing on her rheumatic
fingers as she played. She wrote poetry too, and I still play and sing one
of her poems put to music by a friend, a tearfully sentimental song
called "September," the punch line being "Sometimes I *know* you must
remember that September day!"

Perhaps the most dramatic of my Hollidaysburg memories happened
when I was three years old. Judge Baldridge, who lived next door to
Grandmother's house on Allegheny Street, always carried a pocketful of
penny-sized peppermints especially popular with little girls. On that
fateful morning of September 6, 1901, I saw him on the brick sidewalk
outside the iron fence. I slipped through the gate and coyly sidled up to
him, already tasting the hoped-for peppermints. A friend approached
the judge and stopped him. The two old gentlemen's heads were high
up in that unreachable grown-up region. But I distinctly heard the words
that exploded from the friend's mouth. "The President has been
assassinated!" Whether I knew what "assassinated" meant did not matter.
Something dreadful had happened. It was suddenly as if the sun had
gone out and the whole grown-up world was wrapped in an evil,
menacing cloud. Frightened, I ran back into the house to find my
mother.

*   *   *

Very different from our visits to Hollidaysburg were our yearly trips
to South Carolina. But reaching Belvidere Plantation where father's
sister Aunty Sinkler and Uncle Charley lived was a complicated matter.
The plantation was sixty miles north of Charleston and even reaching it
by train involved a train ride to Pregnalls, a junction where we waited

3

for hours. Another train of two cars took us to Eutawville where we were met by a horse and buggy from the plantation. Then came the long drive on public roads to the Belvidere gates, and soon we were splashing through the Eutaw Springs where the famous battle of that name was fought in the Revolutionary War, and driving another mile or so to the big house. I can remember my first visit when I was about four years old because we were put into a large room with six windows and a big fireplace adjacent to the main house. Father and Mother slept in a huge fourposter bed so high up one had to use steps to get into it. Eleanor and I shared another bed in a corner, and my baby brother, St. Julien, slept in a trundle bed that was pushed under the double bed in the daytime. Each morning, before anyone was out of bed, an old mammy would enter the bedroom, light the fire in the fireplace and set a large oval tin tub in front of it. She would then go out and bring back two large kettles of boiling water. One by one, Eleanor and I stood in the tub, freezing on one side, and scorching on the other while Mother gave us our baths. I learned early that we must be exactly on time for breakfast to line up with the whole household, servants included, while Uncle Charlie read morning prayer. To be one minute late was to be in disgrace.

Year after year, waking up at Belvidere was a joy. Cozily in bed with a fire sparkling on the hearth, you listened to blue jays, red birds, doves, the voluble outburst of song from the Carolina wren, and high above them all the loud *peeto-peeto-peeto* of the titmice. All at once there was another sound below your window—a flock of sheep released from their pen, being driven down the lawn to where they were to graze that day, lambs bleating, bells tinkling, feet tramping, the clamor growing fainter as they passed by.

Life back at Chestnut Hill was very different, but I always enjoyed coming home, and a particular incident occurred at just about this age of four or five which influenced my entire attitude toward life. After we children had gone to bed Mother used to play the piano night after night. I have often wondered if the whole world would not be a better place if every child could grow up being lulled to sleep in an aura of beauty, harmony and rhythm. I still have three volumes of her *Choice Classics for the Piano* published in Boston, 1887, which contain wonderful lyrical pieces such as the *Barcarole, Murmuring Zephyrs, Traumerei, Moment Musicale* and *The Dance of the Sylphs.*

She started each one of us children with piano lessons. My older sister fell by the way and my younger brother didn't take to it at all. But for me it was very different. By the time I was four years old I had mastered

4

a simple five finger exercise played in the key of C with two hands an octave apart. On one particular occasion my mother, seated beside me on the long piano stool, told me to play this again very slowly. She then accompanied me in the bass with soft rich chords, each one changing to harmonize with the successive notes. The result filled my whole being with an inner joy and thrill impossible to describe. Not until years later did I encounter Goethe's words "a poet loves beauty because his emotions respond to harmony with exquisite gladness." I was too young for such adept words but that "moment musicale" opened to me a whole world of inspiration, wonder and delight, and from then on piano playing and music in general became a normal part of my life.

Perhaps it was only natural that after the *Mother Goose* years of light verse, and Robert Louis Stevenson's *A Child's Garden of Verse* I found similar inspiration in poetry, assisted no doubt by my Father's present on my fourteenth birthday—a copy of *The Golden Treasury*. In it he wrote a description instructing me to read it "for the adornment of my mind" and "the cultivation of an appreciation of English letters." It was not long before the names of Wordsworth, Milton, Tennyson, Shelley, Keats and Blake became as familiar to me as Chopin, Grieg, Schumann, Sibelius, Brahms and Debussy.

Inevitably the pattern of our childhood world changed as we grew older. Some of the boys went to boarding school—St. Paul's, Exeter Academy, Groton, and the girls to Westover or Rosemary Hall. But the greatest change for our family occurred when I was eleven. My father had bought about an acre of land from Dr. Woodward on the "wrong side of the tracks," a new road above Casey's Pond (now Lincoln Drive) which was called Navajo Street. Our house, on a rise of ground, was the first new house to be built in that neighborhood. It was a beautiful house of white plaster with black shutters and French windows opening on terraces, and two pie-shaped porches, one covered, the other under a pergola on which my father, a lover of gardens, grew an exotic vine which bore pale yellow blossoms facing downwards instead of reaching for the sun. There was a trellis and big wooden gateway to screen off the kitchen yard from a sunken garden enclosed in hedges and a high stone wall.

We children were ecstatic, each with a large bedroom to ourselves, and the word "home" took on an enriched meaning. Opposite the dining room across a spacious hallway was father's study which he forbade anyone to refer to as a den. He drew an imaginary line across the wide doorway over which we children were forbidden to step unless invited. Naturally when he wasn't around we disobeyed and to this day when I

5

enter that room an echoing ripple of guilt runs up my spine. The Henry Reaths have lived there now for over thirty years and have made adaptations which in my opinion have been improvements.

What I did not like about my new bedroom was a list my father called "Regulations for Mary," which he thumb-tacked on the inside of my bedroom door. But as I grew older I could understand his wish to set me on the right track of an orderly life, nor did I think of this at the time as a form of tyranny. I just didn't want to be "regulated."

REGULATIONS FOR MARY

Rise at 7 o'clock in the morning, wash and dress quickly, without playing with cats or anything else, and without reading. Do not go beyond the bathroom door until dressed.

Bathroom hours in the morning
Eleanor, 6:50 o'clock
Mary and St. Julien, 7:10 o'clock.

Meal-times
Breakfast, 7:50
Lunch, 1:30
Dinner, 6:30

Dining Room and Meals
Come to table promptly and quickly, display good manners and politeness.

Retire at 7:45 in the evening. Look around in the sitting-room and hall at 7:40, and gather up all books, games, coats, hats, etc., and put them in their places, say good-night, and go to your room at once. Retire without reading or playing. Do not call down to your mother or anyone else except to let her know you are ready for bed. Be quiet and make no noise. Do not go beyond the bathroom door.

Piano Practice
One hour per day after lunch, except Wednesday and Saturday and Sunday.

Study Period at Home
Begin to study lessons for the next day at 5 o'clock P.M.,—that is, be at your study table at 5 o'clock, except Saturday and Sunday.

Rest Period
Lie down fifteen to twenty minutes after each study period, and before dinner.

General Orderliness
Put hats, coats, books, playthings, rubbers, etc., away in their places at once when you come into the house; do not let them lie around in the halls, on tables or chairs, floors, etc. Keep your room and clothes neat and in order. "Have a place for everything and everything in its place," so that you can get them when needed, even in the dark.

Sunday is to be a holy day and to be made different from the other days
of the week, not a day for amusements or visiting but to be devoted
to sacred things and your family.

As I record with affection my parents' determination to bring me up
properly, I look back and marvel at the general light-heartedness of my
childhood. Temperamentally I was impatient and given to tantrums
when I didn't get my own way, or if the weather insulted me by raining
the day of a hockey game, thus forcing it to be postponed. And I had
my share of mumps, chicken pox, clipped tonsils and whooping cough,
as well as inescapable nasty jealousies in sports and "unfair" episodes
when denied what I considered my rights. But on the whole, spared
from shyness or any serious feelings of guilt (unless I knew I'd done
something mean) I went "singing down the years" interested in everything
that went on about me.

No one who lives long enough can avoid reaching what Joseph Conrad
described as "the shadow-line," that moment between childhood and
the awakening of manhood. For me that moment stands out clearly. It
happened at Pinelands Camp, a summer camp for girls on Squam Lake
in New Hampshire run by Mrs. Adolpho Muñoz and her three daughters:
Miss Marìa Dalton (from a former marriage) and Miss Inès and Miss
Adela. From the start I had been impressed with the way they handled
the sports. Form was as important as speed. Form and grace in handling
paddles or oars, or drifting over a hurdle or throwing a discus, were just
as important as crossing over a finish line first. Pinelands' standards were
high, and those of us who had been there before loved it. But camp life
had gotten off to a bad start that summer because it rained for three
weeks and outdoor activities were impossible. There were no canoe
picnics, no mountain climbing, no field sports, and training crews for
Crew Day, the big day of the year, were curtailed.

One day Miss Dalton rounded up five of us "old" girls and put it up
to us. Where was our Pinelands spirit? Just huddling together and talking
about the old days wasn't helping the gloomy situation. The counselors
couldn't do everything and the new girls would never love Pinelands the
way we did if *we* didn't do something about it. We had never been more
surprised in our young lives! We were being challenged into some sort
of responsibility—introduced, as it were, into seeing a situation close to
our own interests from the eyes of the grown-ups. All at once we *were*
grownups! And what fun we had, feeling important as we organized
games, treasure hunts, and idiotic skits for the stage! Fortunately the
weather changed and the tottering Pinelands spirit survived.

Several of us went home that September feeling we'd graduated into

7

a higher class, and I didn't mind considering myself a "youngster" for that was a grown-up term, but I was decidedly no longer a child. This new sense of self-awareness asserted itself at once. I decided I didn't want to go to Bryn Mawr College after all. Mary Tyler and I, the two last pupils to graduate from Wissahickon Heights School, had passed our entrance examinations, and she signed herself up as a college freshman. I was tired of rules and regulations and of being surrounded by women. I wanted to explore what lay "outside there in the real world." Unfortunately my parents did not see it that way and I agreed to go to Dana Hall for one year, a post-graduate school in Wellesley, Massachusetts. I learned a great deal there and had excellent teachers in English, French, physics and history of art. Especially fine was my music teacher, Madame Doane. But war broke out in Europe and soon its shadow was beginning to reach us. The Chestnut Hill boys we'd grown up with were disappearing into training camps and my sister Eleanor's marriage to Butler Windle, a young lawyer in West Chester, Pennsylvania, was a big event in our family life. Soon after their wedding, Butler enlisted in the Judge Advocate's Department of Pennsylvania's Twenty-eighth Division and was sent to Augusta, Georgia before duties overseas in France.

The home fires were kept burning by many service groups, and the Chestnut Hill branch of the National League of Women's Services opened headquarters at 8419 Germantown Avenue, their volunteers working at surgical dressings classes and repairing soldiers' clothes. Perhaps nothing at Chestnut Hill could have interested me at that time because what I really wanted was to become an air pilot, but women could not join the active military forces. It was not the first time I wished I were a man, and frequently I dressed like one, wearing Norfolk jackets and a man's dark green velour hat cocked at what I thought a rakish angle. I would have worn trousers if it had been the custom for the so-called gentler sex. How difficult I must have made life for my parents!

If I couldn't become an aviator at least I could get into uniform, and I joined the emergency Aid Aides, a service group with headquarters in town at the Bellevue Stratford Annex. How proud we girls were in our tailored dark blue uniforms with the letters EAA in red on our sleeves and lapels, how military our Sam Browne belts! The corps was organized on a strictly military fashion from privates to generals. Our duties were to man the Liberty Loan booths being erected all over town and collect clothes and food to be sent overseas. The latter was stored, listed and packed up in the Wanamaker store rooms. On the main floor near the famous Wanamaker Bronze Eagle, a popular Liberty Loan booth was erected where military officers from England, France, Australia and Canada, men who had been discharged from active service because of wounds, made speeches urging people to buy bonds.

I rose from private to inspecting sergeant and loved the three red chevrons on my left sleeve. I loved my job, too. It took me all over town making the round of hospitals, store rooms and Liberty Loan booths to see that each day's volunteers were actually on the job, and to report those who hadn't turned up. I was driven all over the city from Kensington to the Navy yard—which helped me years later in my political work to know my Philadelphia.

It was at the Bronze Eagle that I met a Canadian captain who became a great friend. He often came out to 7708 Navajo Street and was loved by all of us. Butler Windle was overseas and Eleanor was again staying with us and the captain became quite one of the family. We realized that many, many men who had seen active service found it difficult to settle down to the pattern of their former lives, and our captain was one of them. He had survived the Battle of Vimy Ridge, and had fearful memories that haunted him, as well as a piece of shrapnel in his back that frequently troubled him. I can now understand how his visits to quiet Chestnut Hill were a blessing to him. Years later we heard he had become a distinguished heart specialist in Toronto.

In the spring of 1918, twelve of the EA Aides volunteered to train as nurses' aides at the Protestant Episcopal Hospital, 2nd and Front Streets. I was one of them. I got up early each morning, put on my nurse's uniform, had breakfast, slipped into a dark blue cape lined with red, slapped on my overseas cap with the correct tilt and walked to St. Martin's Station to catch the 7:21 train to town. At North Philadelphia I would get off and catch a trolley down to Front Street. Sometimes a troop train would pause at North Philadelphia, every window jammed with dough-boys leaning out and calling, "Hey, Nurse! Come here! I'm sick!"

All through that hot and desperate summer we were given menial jobs at the hospital. We washed dirty windowsills, carried trays, put away clean linen in geometrical precise piles in the closet room and learned how to make "square corners" on the beds. If they weren't perfect the head nurse would come along, rip them up and make you do it all over again. We graduated after a month to washing patients and taking our turn in different wards. The surgical wards weren't so bad, but the medical wards were terrible; even worse, the baby wards. I could hardly stand that. But we survived and were sent all about town during the influenza epidemic to hospitals that were in distress because many doctors and nurses were absent, down with the flu. We found dressingrooms in

9

frightful disorder and were forced to hand bottles with smeared labels to the interns in charge. Hospital corridors everywhere were lined with bodies waiting to be removed to make room for more and more of the dying.

Then came that early morning of the official Armistice Day! There had been a false one a few days before, but this was the real thing! Whistles began to blow and bells to ring—church bells, fire bells, auto horns! I rushed into Eleanor's room and in that early dawn we hugged each other, danced around, wept and kept repeating "The killing's over! The killing's over!" All at once we recognized the familiar sound of the bells of St. Martin's played in a helter-skelter joyous abandon, the notes just tumbling all over themselves! Later we learned it was young Chandler Ross who had flung on his clothes and rushed to the church, managed to climb up the bell tower—no mean feat—and had begun pulling ropes.

The "flu" epidemic wore itself out and the boys from "over there" began drifting home. Eleanor left 7708 again and went back to West Chester when Butler returned. My brother graduated from Haverford School and, being of a scientific nature, entered Drexel University. In June of 1919, the Emergency Aid Aides were disbanded on one of the hottest days on record. Impressive ceremonies took place at Lindenwold, Mr. John Wanamaker's estate in Jenkintown, and were presided over by General Price, of the Pennsylvania National Guard. The nurses' aides who had helped through the influenza epidemic were awarded small, cherished medals.

My final contact with the military occurred a year or so later at the Mardi Gras Ball in New Orleans when I danced with General Pershing. We were permitted to cut in on him—a new custom in ballroom etiquette considered barbarous by the older generation, but we girls made the most of it. You couldn't waltz the general halfway around the ballroom floor without some other damsel cutting in on him, and how he loved it! The war was over and he was home again and they say he danced with over seventy girls that night!

So we all packed away our uniforms in dusty attic trunks and began to realize that nothing would ever be the way it used to be. Back home in Chestnut Hill we could not help but notice that all sorts of changes were taking place around us. We no longer had to run into town for everything—dentists, oculists, fancy groceries at Fluke's Store on Chestnut Street, clothes and shoes at Gimbles, Wanamakers, Strawbridge and Clothier and Lit Brothers because our community began to expand commercially and professionally. And Dr. Woodward began to build his

French and English "villages," courts, and byways, setting a high tone in architecture and an agreeable way of life.

But there were other basic facts which, from the beginning, made our community destined for distinction. The Wissahickon Valley, described by Baedeker as "a miniature Alpine gorge" and its tributaries like the stream down Rex and Chestnut Hill avenues, and the Cresheim Creek, played an important part in making us what we are today—a historic district recorded in the National Register. The easy access to this natural environment affected the entire population, from opulent residents living in what David Eichler likes to call "mansions" to green-grocers, stone-masons, plumbers, and contractors living in smaller houses—the some-bodies and the nobodies. All have enjoyed, shoulder to shoulder, skating on the dark green ice of the Wissahickon, coasting down Springfield Avenue to Valley Green, fishing in spring, riding horseback, bicycling, picking violets, blood-root and buttercups in the sheltered meadows beside the Cresheim Creek. The result was inevitable: the fashioning of a community spirit of caring, of belonging, and of sharing something rare and beautiful, free to all.

Chapter 2

1920–1930

THE PLEASANT RHYTHM of pre-war life was considerably shaken up by the plunge into that famous decade known under many headings—"The Jazz Age," "The Roaring Twenties," "The Lawless Decade." Disrupting forces ran the gamut from votes for women; prohibition; the "family car" (which changed our lifestyle more than anyone expected); the first daily network of broadcasting daily news over the radio with Lowell Thomas as commentator; magnificent silent movies with Garbo, Billie Burke, Clark Gable, Humphrey Bogart and "Mickey Mouse," to Gershwin's "Rhapsody in Blue," Lindbergh's flight across the Atlantic, Teapot Dome, the Florida boom, and a broken Woodrow Wilson.

Something else happened which added considerable complications to my personal life. I fell in love with a Yale man who lived in a far-away midwestern city well off the familiar social pattern of my Atlantic coastline flyway. He was the cousin of a friend I had made at Pinelands, and I met him at her house over a weekend house-party. He became my measuring rod for all men for years to come, our experience a pattern of confused youthfulness and intense attraction which neither of us learned how to handle. In those days we did not use the words "boyfriend" or "ladyfriend" which today frequently means living together without marriage and exploring that wonderful world of intimacy which in my time was taboo without a marriage license tucked away among glowing photographs of ecstatic bride, groom, parents, relatives and friends. We used the word "beau" for the male who was openly attentive to a special female, and today's expression "dating," which falls unpleasantly on my ears, did not exist. What's more, a girl of my day gloried in how many beaux she could collect, sometimes dividing them into categories such as "my horseback riding beau"; my "tennis beau" or a beau (usually an "older man" with more money than a mere boy) who took her to the theatre after dinner at the Ritz! As soon as a girl decided on the man of her dreams and they became openly engaged, her retinue dropped away instantaneously and she faced the complicated but much desired status of a married woman.

I never considered my Yale man a "beau." He lived way out yonder toward Wisconsin except when at college and never became part of the Philadelphia picture. I saw him at New Haven football games; once at the Yale "Prom," the last "Prom" before we entered World War I. He left for France as a second lieutenant and returned as a captain. We saw each other only twice thereafter, each time fatally misunderstanding each other. I have often asked myself how could a person you never really *knew* influence your whole life for years to come? Of course we wrote to each other for awhile and seven years later he married. I "carried on" with music and writing and took up an interest in world affairs sparked by Miss Ellen Gowen Hood. She was that rare being, a Chestnut Hill Democrat, who wanted to "do her bit" in helping the United States play a part in "making the world safe for Democracy."

Philadelphia was ninety-nine percent Republican at that time, but even later when the Democrats were in control, the big power boys in both city committees were never able to predict the Chestnut Hill vote, referring to us as "those confounded ticket-splitters up there in the 22nd ward." Indeed, the Chestnut Hill community has provided the city with the highest number of distinguished lawyers, judges, doctors, professors, senators and mayors of any other portion of the city; also in the Clark and Dilworth days, the first woman in the City Concil, Constance S. Dallas.

With the help of a friend—Miss Mary Archer of Reading, Pennsylvania—Miss Hood rounded up an astonishing number of ladies in and about Philadelphia who also wanted to back up the League of Nations, and the Democratic Women's Luncheon Club was born. Miss Hood enrolled some of us younger people as well: Eleanor Davis (Mrs. Charles O'Conner) and me from Chestnut Hill; Marion Myers (Mrs. George W. Pepper) and Bessie Downs (Mrs. Rowland Evans) from the Main Line. I became corresponding secretary.

Miss Hood lived across the Cresheim Creek on Gowen Avenue. She was an ardent member of the Philadelphia Cricket Club's golf team, and a shield named in her honor is still a coveted inter-club trophy. Although fighting for the League of Nations was a different sort of challenge from winning a golf trophy, the Democratic Women's Luncheon Club flourished for a dozen years organizing a program of luncheons held at the Bellevue Stratford. The speeches were printed at the club's expense and mailed to what became a membership in over forty states. No doubt many of our Republican friends smiled condescendingly at the aims of the club, if they even knew it existed, and rgarded us as a harmless group of dear little ladies who believed that Woodrow Wilson was a hero deserving of a halo. But top flight VIP statesmen from the president's cabinet did not indulge in this kind of male chauvinism. In fact, it tickled the fancy of such distinguished gentlemen as Carter Glass, Newton Baker, Josephus Daniels and John W. Davis to broadcast Democratic principles in the very heart of Republican Philadelphia. And they did it without pay!

Meanwhile our overseas forces drifted home from Europe and I watched my friends marry and start their families. Apparently destiny had something else in store for me, but I spent many agonizing hours walking in the Wissahickon and the Cresheim Valley wondering what on earth to do with myself. More than once I decided to kick over the traces, abandon little old Chestnut Hill and join the ranks of flaming youth in Greenwich Village, New York. But flappers, raccoon coats, hip-pocket flasks, cloche hats and free verse without capital letters couldn't measure up against a new Steinway grand piano my parents had given me, the "family car," and "passes" over the entire Pennsylvania Railroad system, including Pullman.

I tried to work up a musical ambition and was accepted by the matinee Musical Club in Philadelphia after performing Brahm's *Second Rhapsody in G Minor* in a manner acceptable to the club's membership committee. I was soon shocked by the bitter jealousies and fierce competition for the limelight among my fellow pianists, realized I did not have what it takes to become a professional, and resigned from the club. Music was sacred to me, a source of inspiration, and the undeniable evidence that beauty, rhythm and harmony make it worthwhile to try to live some sort of a decent, useful life.

I know my mother was worried about me, and that she wanted me to marry a fine young man, settle down and have a family. Theoretically I wanted to find that young man too, but I had weak maternal instincts and "family life" was not my main objective at that moment. She gave me Will Durant's *Story of Philosophy* and I flung myself into a self-education project of filling notebooks with wise quotations from poets and philosophers. I also became absorbed in a book called *Studies in Idealism* by Hugh L'Anson Fausset. He wrote, "Reason is used to induce order out of divided sensation," which I privately translated as meaning the brain is the steering wheel and emotion is the engine. One notebook was packed with the sayings of Marcus Aurelius. My temperament was a fierce mixture of desire and impatience. More than ever did I want to

15

reach out beyond my family and circle of friends to a wider companionship with people who thought, appreciated, and enjoyed what I did.

The result of all this was the writing of what I called a "tone poem" entitled *Duragon* or *The Search for Companionship.* This told the story of a restless young god who leaves Mount Olympus to seek a special kind of companionship that could not be found among the gods. The writing style was something like the sing-song found in parts of the King James version of the Bible. The manuscript holds interest for forty odd pages, then drones on and becomes boring. I never have sent it to a publisher.

This headlong stampede into the world of philosophy was interrupted by my parents' decision to send me to Europe in a small group, properly chaperoned. We set sail in mid-January for Italy on the litte White Star liner *Arabic.* Up until this adventure I had been within reach of a piano to ease the spirit regardless of mood—*fortissimo, furioso, andante, allegro,* or *doloroso.* Travel abruptly cut me off from this safety valve; after eleven days on a gray and stormy Atlantic Ocean, the sudden sunlight on a mass of purple bougainvillea festooned over the palisades of Funchal, Madeira, sent me into paroxysms of joy and I burst into a sonnet to Funchal. From then on, during the six months I was in Europe, I exploded into verse and on my return home, I sent the Funchal sonnet to the *Evening Bulletin* and it appeared on the editorial page on February 27, 1923. The very next day a letter signed "E. Biddle" praising the sonnet also appeared on the editorial page. My excitement was two-fold: to see in print what had sprung from the privacy of my mind filled me with that sensation Marcus Aurelius described as "self-satisfaction"—not a smug feeling by any means, but one of having taken the first step toward my objective—a direct contact with persons unknown "out there in the wide, wide world."

In the meantime I discovered that just about everybody was writing poetry, all of us vying with each other to get our passionate emotions immortalized in the *Saturday Review of Literature,* Harriet Monroe's *Poetry,* Henry Goddard Leach's *Forum,* and right at home in Philadelphia Charles Wharton Stork's *Contemporary Verse.*

On my next visit to Charleston I fell into a nest of poets and a highly literary atmosphere. I had always thought Charleston men were more attractive than the Philadelphia youths with whom I had grown up. The southerners, even those of my own age, were men, while the Philadelphia males were still adolescents, heading for the law, banking, industrial careers (all very important but not inspiring). Of course, the same ambitions were stirring in the Charleston men but the latter had something

16

else besides: They knew their land. Plantation life was still alive and no male Charlestonian was ashamed or considered himself prissy or effete to know the difference between a Carolina wren and a house wren, or the names of flowering shrubs and vines in the magnificent gardens of Middleton and Magnolia Plantations. In the fall and winter they hunted quail, turkey, duck and deer. In short, they were countrymen at heart. I liked the way they dressed over week-ends in corduroy jackets and trousers tucked into riding boots. Also they knew how to make a girl feel desirable and at the same time to understand that their *at*-tentions were not necessarily *in*-tentions! There really is a great deal to be said in favor of the art of flirting!

The Charleston poets I knew best were DuBose Heyward, Hervey Allen and Josephine Pinckney. This was before DuBose abandoned his legal profession for writing. His greatest work of course was his creation of Porgy. Nor had Hervey Allen as yet written *Anthony Adverse,* nor Josephine her *Three O'Clock Dinner.* Together DuBose and Hervey had published a slim book of poetry called *Carolina Chansons,* and Josephine was to bring out shortly her *Sea-Drinking Cities.* Poetry books were appearing across the country from such writers as Edna St. Vincent Millay, Sara Teasdale and Amy Lowell. In New York City, Henry Seidel Canby, Amy Loveman, William Rose Benèt and Christopher Morley flocked together and established a literary review for the New York Evening Post—predecessor to what became *The Saturday Review of Literature.* Every poet aimed at having a poem appear in the SRL, and, as more literary birds joined the flock, a group began meeting for lunch at the Algonquin Hotel to discuss their failures and successes, the eccentricities of publisher's editorials, good and bad reviewing, and the difference between reviewing and criticism. A large round table was reserved for them in the rear dining room, and many a time when in New York, alone or with friends, I'd make a beeline for a table in that room and bask in the delicious atmosphere created by these literary giants—"figures against the sky" as Cornelius Weigandt used to describe them in an English class I attended at the University of Pennsylvania one winter. For the next fifty years members of *The Algonquin-Round Table* had a strong influence on American literature in general.

When in Charleston our family usually stayed with the Stoneys— Cousin Lou and Cousin Sam and their four children, Gus, Sam, Louisa and Harriet—and Faber, their butler and general factotum, a man of great dignity. The Stoney Plantation, Medway, was much nearer Charleston than Belvidere and I was thrilled with the wild way Sam and Gus drove their cars over corduroy roads through the swamps or along

17

hard sandy beaches. They were like older brothers to me and were also not only literary-minded but well-versed in geneology. Knowing who you are and where you came from is one of Charleston's favorite pastimes, and the Sam Stoney of my generation became *the* authority on Charleston's historic past and complicated family relationships. Sam overflowed with anecdotes, had a wicked sense of humor, a glint in his eye, grew a Van Dyke beard like my father's and informed me that back in the 1880's there had been three "dashing young Sams" in Charleston—his father Sam Stoney, my father Sam Porcher, and their cousin Sam Gaillard, the latter by far the handsomest of the three.

It is not the purpose of the present auto-history to delve deeply into geneology, but the story of the offspring of these three dashing Sams tells how and why the lasting ties between Charleston and Philadelphia go on from generation to generation. For example: Cousin Sam Stoney sent his two daughters Harriet and Louise to board at Springside School in Chestnut Hill. They made many friends in Philadelphia, but married Charleston men. Harriet's son, however, married Virginia Cooke, daughter of Philadelphian M.T. Cooke, and they live in Chestnut Hill today. At another time, when Cousin Sam Gaillard and Cousin Lynch were living here they sent their sons Ned and Dine (Gourdin) to the Chestnut Hill Academy, and thence on to Yale University, where they both fell in love and married "damn Yankee" maidens from New England. As for my father Sam Porcher, he married a northerner, and his two daughters did likewise. My brother never married at all. And so it will continue I suspect, many happy relationships between the two cities seeping into the generations below mine.

Because I am one of the half-and-halves I waver at times between my loyalties, and because comparisons are odious I try to be tactful. But secretly I think "southern hospitality" is, shall we say, a very special type of hospitality. For example, I remember a visit to Charleston with my father when I was about eighteen. He had arranged to take my brother down for a few days, but St. J fell ill and I was taken in his place. The Palmetto Limited delivered us at our destination at the familiar early hour and we went directly to the Villa Margharita on the South Battery for breakfast. Father was suffering from unpredictable headaches at this time and did not like to impose himself on any of our cousins' households. Halfway through breakfast a tall black man, hat in hand, approached our table. He was Faber, the Stoney's butler, very much distressed that we were not staying at cousin Sam's Tradd Street house. He had come to offer us his services just as if we were there.

It turned out that on the following night the St. Cecilia Ball was to

18

take place, an institution that vied with Philadelphia's Assembly in being the oldest social affair of its kind in the country. The formalities of the St. Cecilia to this day remain the same, opening with a cotillion led by the society's president with the bride of the season on his arm. Dance cards are still the order of the day as well as the strict rule of "no cutting in."

Apparently Faber had returned to Tradd Street and informed Cousin Lou of my presence, and before the day was over Louis Parker (who waltzed divinely) presented himself to us at the villa with a dance card, a pretty little thing with a silk cord and tassel in it—already half-filled with the names of some of my partners the following night. I was overcome, and deeply thankful that my mother had packed a party dress in my suitcase. This wasn't my favorite evening dress, but I was presentable. Indeed, I gave Faber a very special smile when he helped me out of the carriage at the door of Hybernian Hall. If this was my first St. Cecilia it was also a big night for him because the St. Cecilia Balls could never be complete without Faber in his coat-tails, high silk hat and white gloves, opening the carriage doors and helping the ladies out in a ceremonious style belonging to him alone.

For a long time I was "little sister" and treated as such by a crowd of older cousins, all three Sinklers—Emily, Anne and Carry, as well as by Josephine Pinckney and my sister Eleanor. Emily was ten years older than I and a very spectacular person. One day when I was about twelve I was seated on her left hand at the dinner table; on her right hand was her "beau" from Boston, a Mr. Wigglesworth. I overheard him say, in a low voice, "Everything you southern girls say sounds like a caress!" Emily replied equally softly, "Perhaps we mean it that way," and a thrill ran through me which made me feel I was seeing life at last!

The day finally arrived when I was no longer little sister. Belvidere was the scene of a weekend house party which included several swains from Charleston—DuBose Heyward, Gus Stoney, Austen Smythe and so forth. This was during my poetry days and I had composed a poem on moss, that gray tangled epiphyte which dangles from great live oaks and other tress, especially in the swamplands. Amy Lowell of Boston once called it "dead men's beards," a remark that did not go down well with the Carolinians. Almost as bad, I had the nerve to write my poem in the Belvidere guest book, taking up a whole page. My Aunty Sinkler thought it charming, and after all it was her guest book, but Josephine jumped down my throat and I discovered that South Carolinians worship Spanish moss. It was a holy thing to them and I had rushed in where angels feared to tread. In fact none of them who had grown up intimately

19

with moss had as yet dared to try to do justice to it in a poem. This I could understand, for there's something eerie, mysterious and hauntingly beautiful about Carolina cypress swamps where it thrives. But after Jo's vituperations I privately chuckled. I was no longer ignored. I had arrived!

DuBose was very gentle about it. In fact, he liked the poem. DuBose was always gentle. Infantile paralysis when he was a child had left his hands crippled, and perhaps it is no wonder that he could create so appealing and memorable a character as the crippled Porgy. Years later, George Gershwin's *Porgy and Bess* overwhelmed me and I still play "Summertime" on the piano but no longer try to sing it.

Up north in Philadelphia, poetry was doing pretty well for itself. A rush of small bookstores began to appear not only in mid-city but in Chestnut Hill and on the Main Line. It became Mr. Charles Wharton Stork's pleasure to choose certain poems from his *Contemporary Verse* and read them at informal meetings in one or another of these shops. In Chestnut Hill, Marion Kingston and Mary Shepherd opened the Fireside Bookshop in a tiny room on Germantown Avenue boasting a real wood burning fireplace. How cozy we were on those red letter days when Mr. Stork read our very own poems, sometimes interpreting them with nuances you, yourself, had not suspected of being there. It is probably because of Mr. Stork that the following event took place on February 17, 1925, when the *Evening Bulletin* reported in this manner:

An Evening with Philadelphia Poets

On February 17, the largest conclave of Philadelphia poets in the history of the city was gathered at the Art Alliance. A large, enthusiastic audience filled the halls and doorways, applauding nearly every poem. The following authors read their own works: Professor Rhys Carpenter, Mary Dixon Thayer, Amory Hare Cook, Mary Borland Thayer, Mac Knight Black, Granville Toogood, John Troth, Robert Spiller, Roy Helton, Gertrude Nason Carver, Virginia McCall, Florence Small, Mary F. Wickham Porcher, Marina Wister, Professor Norryes O'Connor and Phoebe Hoffman. The speakers were introduced by Mr. Charles Wharton Stork.

Also at this time Dorrance and Company of Philadelphia was publishing poems in slender volumes at one dollar apiece in what they called ". . . a sequence representation of the best poetic influence and expression of present day writers. The complete series to day is 35 volumes." Molly Thayer's *New York and Other Poems*, was one of these, likewise Gertrude Nason Carver's *Jupiter's Moons*, Amory Hare's *The Olympians*, and Agnes Hecksher's *Bamboo Curtains*. I was proud when mine appeared in 1926 as *The Tilted Cup*. In it was a sonnet called "The Gift" which

20

was awarded the Philadelphia Browning Society's medal that year. On one side of the medal in bas relief, is *The Rose and the Ring*, and on the other my name and date.

Many writers have started their careers by writing poetry, and I had been told through many sources that if you want to write prose, above all write about something you know *well*. So I cheerfully flung myself into a story for the *St. Nicholas Magazine* about field hockey, for if there was anything I knew something about at this time it was field hockey. Crisp autumn day! Wind swirling leaves! Blue sky above and a flock of migrating grackles. White lines on the green playing ground, and twenty-two girls in bright tunics swinging up and down the field, maneuvering, changing formations. Then a click of ball on hockey sticks, and the "feel" of the ball in control as you dash towards the opponent's goal, dribbling, dodging, quickly passing to your center forward, receiving it back again, and, with a split second glance to keep you from fouling off-side, raising the ball slightly off the ground in your shot to pass the goaler and score. I also knew the locker room politics, and decisions made not on ability but favoritism, and the despair when you'd hoped to play in a certain game but were not called on and had to sit on the sidelines still hoping you'd be out there on the field in the second half.

My story, entitled "Sally Keeps in the Alley" was the first field hockey story to be published in America; the St. Nicholas paid me ninety dollars for it. British women had been playing the game for years and it was introduced into this country in 1904 when Miss Constance Applebee came to Bryn Mawr College as director of physical education. Through her it spread to other women's colleges, and Philadelphia's contribution was to introduce it to country and cricket clubs in the area. A Philadelphia League was formed, with intense competition between teams from Merion, Germantown, Philadelphia Cricket, Lansdowne, and two New Jersey Clubs, Haddonfield and Riverton. Each season the winning team played a well attended game at Bryn Mawr, the latter usually winning. An All-Philadelpia team was chosen and exchanged games with a British team held at the Philadelphia Cricket Club, and once in England. Today there are over three hundred clubs where women's field hockey is played.

Writing about field hockey brought such immediate success financially as well as quick publication I was led to a second attempt, this time with some tennis stories. I was greatly influenced by the Ralph Henry Barbour St. Nicholas stories, matching his titles like "For the Honor of the School" with my "Joanna Plays the Game" and "Sally Keeps in the Alley." My themes were about the little nobody bravely doing the honorable thing instead of grasping for glory. On a certain happy occasion one of my stories appeared side-by-side in the St. Nicholas with one of Ralph Henry Barbour's.

Pretty soon I felt rich enough to tell my father I wanted to spend two weeks at the H F Bar Ranch in Wyoming and could pay for it if he would provide me with railroad passes to get there and home again. He did so, and after a second trip out west—this time to the Double S Ranch in New Mexico—I knew that by now writing was my chosen profession and was encouraged further when one of my tennis stories was translated into Japanese, appearing in a text book for Japanese school children. The next step was to collect these stories and fit them into two books of girls' adventure: *Cherique* (1928) and *Gloom Creek* (1929). Both were published by Appleton-Century just before the Wall Street crash.

My choice of publishers came about in an unexpected fashion. I was sitting in the Palmetto Limited on my way north one spring after a long visit in Charleston and Pinopolis. Sentimental tears were filling my eyes as I regretfully speeded away from the country and style of life I loved so well. Flowing through a Carolina spring there is an undercurrent of glamour and seduction hard to put behind you. Everything is so beautiful—flowers, choruses of birdsong, gardens—Cypress Gardens, Magnolia, Middleton, and the famous little private backyard gardens sprinkled lavishly through the city, each one a miracle of daffodils, rambling roses, tulips, brilliant azalea bushes, tightly furled petals of camellias, and the heavy scent of gardenias and sweet olive. The train was rushing me away from all this and from the feeling of belonging to a long tribe of forebears who had fled persecution in France and undergone together through succeeding generations the settling of new shores and the loves and jealousies of close family ties.

But why weep about it? I was being a sentimental fool and took out my handkerchief to dab my eyes just as a woman older than I crossed the aisle and sat down beside me, saying softly, "Is there any way I can be of help to you?"

Sheepishly I told her I was just being sentimental and, in the conversation that followed, she learned that I had just finished an adventure book for girls—some of the scenes in Charleston—while I found out that she was the daughter of one of the editors in the Appleton-Century publishing house. She made me promise to send my manuscript to her father, and I did so. When they accepted it and I signed the contract for it in their New York offices, I was told, "Now go home and write another."

I did that too, but first decided that, although I had resisted the siren call from Greenwich Village, Virginia Wolfe's idea of a "room of one's own" had grown stronger, and I rented an attic at 1724 Sansom Street in Philadelphia over a shoemaker's shop. For almost a year I revelled in my independence, cheerfully writing my second adventure book for girls and going in and out of town daily, reading Dostoevsky's *The Brothers Karamazov* on the train. I even gave an "After the Opera Party" one night, astonished as I write this that besides my own more intimate friends such distinguished grande dames as Mrs. Edward Browning, Miss Gertrue Ely, and Aunt Caroline Sinkler climbed up two flights of stairs, as well as dear Mr. Harry Brengle and a couple of university professors. Aunt Carry honored the occasion by sending around from her house at 1604 Locust Street a huge potted plant too heavy to carry upstairs but gloriously ostentatious at the top step at the entrance of 1724 Sansom Street. I can't remember what I possibly could have given them to eat or drink.

A Carolina spring may have its powerful enchantments, but so has spring in the Wissahickon. My daily trips back and forth from Sansom Street began to seem like a dreadful waste of time, a problem solved by Dr. Woodward who built for me a little house on the banks of the Cresheim Creek which at first we called "The Meadowhouse," but eventually "The Studio."

Here too were spring flowers of blood-root and anemone, of violets and buttercups, and in the surrounding meadows choruses of fox sparrows, titmice, and, in May, ephemeral songs of warblers passing through on their way to nesting habitats further north. I watched every step of the building of my little house, and, when it was finished and the house-warming party was over, I settled down to attack my first adult novel, which I called *The Vermilion Piano*.

I now have no recollection of what it was about, for something of greater importance occurred: my mother got her wish for me—a fine husband and a settled life. Shippen Lewis and I were married at St. Martin-in-the-Fields on November 19, 1930.

CHAPTER 3

1930–1944

IT WAS AN ODD feeling to leave my father's house at 7708 Navajo Street and to realize it would no longer mean "home." But I moved only a few blocks away to Navajo Street and Hartwell Lane where Shippen lived with his daughters and his sister, Louise Lewis. That section of Navajo Street had its own cozy little atmosphere. There were ten houses on the east side and four on the west, each house proud of itself because of slight variations in architecture, yet all in harmony despite Dr. Woodward's having engaged four different architects—Louis Duhring, Teddy Gilchrist, Bob McGoodwin and, later, Kneedler and Zantzinger.

I knew that Shippen had a great interest in the Civil War and was better informed about it than I, but I didn't expect to visit battle scenes on my wedding trip! However, my contribution to the situation was our visit to an elderly cousin, Senator Henry T. Wickham who lived at Hickory Hill twenty miles outside Richmond near Hanover Court, home of Patrick Henry. Shippen was gratifyingly impressed with the loveliness of the plantation and he and Cousin Henry found much to talk about. I left them to their conversation about battles that had been fought around Hickory Hill and wandered around outside remembering how our father had brought us children down at one time or another to visit our Wickham relations at Shirley and Lower Brandon on the James River.

Here at Hickory Hill was where my grandmother Mary Fanning Wickham grew up—"May Fan" as she was called—and where she and her sister Lucy were married in a double wedding. This was temporarily postponed by a blizzard, and the two bridegrooms, Julius Theodore Porcher from Charleston, and George Harrison Byrd from New York City, were unable to reach Hickory Hill for three days. Another cousin, Thomas Nelson Page, told us he had always wanted to write a story about this—the excitement and anxiety inside the big house crowded

25

with bridesmaids and relatives. But he never "got around to it." As I wandered about the property, I too tried to picture what those three chaotic days might have been like.

The lawn around the house was like a park, the feature of the garden a long walk of boxwood trees planted in 1820, now thirty feet high. Similar to South Carolina plantations were the "out-houses," the kitchen and laundry in a long wooden building, an orangery, and the office, a two-story building where the business of the plantation could be arranged by members of the family and the plantation overseer. Further away from the big house, down the lawn, was the library, a small cottage to which Cousin Henry, like his father and grandfather, withdrew daily to his books, his law and his reading.

After our wedding trip was over we returned home to Chestnut Hill. As for "settling down" in my mother's terms, my new life was the embodiment of the old maxim "variety is the spice of life." Along with having found the companionship I had longed for, there were three girls—Louise, aged nine, Polly, thirteen and Dora, fifteen. Their mother had died four years previously and Shippen's sister Louise Lewis had come to live with them. I had not given much thought to the prospect of becoming a stepmother, but had been warned by my mother that I could not correct or chastise my stepdaughters until I had built up a friendly relationship with each one separately. All of us were realistic enough not to act as if I were their mother, so they called me by my first name. I regarded them as younger sisters, and as all of them were exceptionally pretty as well as intelligent, I didn't think there would be much trouble.

True, Dora went through a phase when she complained about feeling unwell to go to school one morning, but by lunch time when Foxy and Coxey dropped in to inquire about her, Dora was quite well enough to join them and whatever her crowd had planned for the afternoon. After this happened a couple of times I caught on to the maneuver, and, on another day when Dottie and Betty showed up at the front door, I explained that Dora was not well, nothing serious, but could not come downstairs today. The girls left, and Dora missed catching up on the latest news about what "everybody" was doing. There were no more school morning fade-outs.

Polly gave us a little trouble with her warm-hearted friendliness, treating her friends lavishly on their way home from school to sodas and sundaes at Streeper's drug store. Not only did our bill leap to surprising figures but Polly's frequent night-time colly-wobbles seemed to occur after these congenial gatherings. True to her fondness for people and food she blossomed into a charming hostess. After almost twenty years in Baltimore, and a divorce, she returned to Chestnut Hill. With James Eiseman, her second husband, she became known for her elegant table and hospitality, especially at Christmas-time, when nieces, nephews, in-laws, children, grand-children and stepmother were gathered together under one roof.

As for "Weezie," she and I were too much alike, both with strong beliefs in our own points of view and an explosive readiness to declare them. But I loved them all and they taught me a great deal. Also they had their innings. Their great-aunt, Aunt Anna Shippen Lewis, who lived at 22nd and Sansom Streets, gave me a beautiful necklace of amethysts with earrings to match for a wedding present. I had nothing suitable to wear with them, so I bought some lavender crêpe de chine and had a dressmaker create a lovely evening dress, not a ball gown. The first time I wore it, amethysts and all, I came downstairs and found the girls in the hall. We all enjoyed seeing each other dressed up for a party, but before I'd reached the bottom step they began to giggle. I could not see why. I was trying to look composed and dignified but they kept on looking at me and giggling. It turned out that I had floated down the stairs with what they considered a *la-di-da* smile, as if trying to look like the Queen of Roumania. But *they* weren't going to be fooled! *They* knew me inside out and thereafter never missed referring, when they thought it appropriate, to what they dubbed my "amethyst smile." Sometimes three against one just isn't fair!

And there we all were with Aunt Lou just across the hedge in a new house she had built on Woodward property which became 8030 Navajo Street. No one could have had a more tactful and understanding sister-in-law than I did. We were in and out of her house as much as she was in and out of ours. Shippen of course was the kingpin, with a veritable "harem" of females about him. I had to share him with his father's sister Aunt Anna, his mother's sister Aunt Esther Bradford who lived in Chestnut Hill, his own sister Louise, and his three daughters. His brother, Dr. Robert M. Lewis, lived with his entourage in New Haven, Connecticut.

Recently a young man who naturally could not have known Shippen asked me one day "What sort of man was he—really?" I could not have told him in the 1930s other than the obvious, that Shippen Lewis at forty-three was a handsome, distinguished-looking lawyer in the law firm of MacCoy, Evans, Hutchinson and Lewis with quantities of friends— a man who at first meeting you knew would never let you down. I could add that he had gone to the Delancey School in Philldelphia, graduating at the age of fifteen. His father had died in a train accident when he was three years old, and, at fifteen, his mother considered him too young to enter college. So she sent him off to a ranch school in California where the boys were made to take care of their horses, make their own bunks and be exposed to other practical matters. I always believed this experience saved Shippen from becoming a "stuffy" highbrow Phildelphia lawyer, and he agreed with me!

After finishing college at the University of Pennsylvania and the Law School he married Esther Emlen and lived in Awbury Park, Germantown, among many of her Quaker cousins, the Copes, the Emlens and the Scattergoods. Here the three girls were born, and at their mother's death he moved his family to Chestnut Hill, where his sister Louise came to live with them.

Should I again meet that young man who wanted to know what Shippen was "really like" I could now add that he must have been something special the day he was born, for he grew up with a clear mind under control, motivated by supremely humanistic concerns. He made an art of personal relationships. It was fascinating to watch how his mind worked.

He could meet his subordinates, raise them to his own level, then treat them as equals. He could find something to respect in almost everyone he encountered, and translated "charity" and "loving one's neighbor" into "good will." I watched him time and again in a meeting of minds on occasions when hostility and vituperation threatened, analyzing the argument quickly, clearly, and often with humor. This did not always result in agreement by any means, but because he turned the spotlight on what was obviously reasonable to the majority those who refused to accept that as fact, lost face.

During World War II he was the hearing officer for the Department of Justice in cases of conscientious objectors, as well as an arbitrator for the National War Labor Board. Later he was proposed for the Superior Court, a Federal Judgeship, and by Francis Biddle, Attorney General, for the Supreme Court in Washington. A serious heart attack a few years after our marriage would have made the latter impossible for him.

It was also fascinating to watch how he handled his daughters when they erred and strayed. They found his silences more powerful and "scary" than any spoken words could convey. In other words, knowing that they knew they had misbehaved he quietly gave them time to acknowledge it. As for me, he soon learned of my quick and impatient temperament, inherited (partly) from my volatile Huguenot ancestors.

For example, he could take the side of the policeman who had caught me speeding or running through a red light, and not make me furious.

Sometimes I think of those days in the 1930s as my "engraved invitation days," for within ten years we had three coming-out parties and three weddings, as well as formal dinner parties before the Assembly or theatre parties. It was a delightful period for me. I loved the girls and all the gaiety around them, and became familiar with the maitre d's at the Ritz, the Bellevue, the Warwick, and the various country clubs. It was the whimsical "in" thing at the time for those who gave the really grandest affairs to refer to the ball as a "small dance at ten o'clock." But do not be deceived. Were the affair to take place on the top floor of the Bellevue known as The Rose Garden, you would make a social *faux pas* if you did not wear a white tie and tails, and the ladies, their very, very best ball gowns. I remember one of these occasions when the motif was something between a horse show and a fox hunt. Paddocks had been built on the roof garden of the Bellevue, the floors inside covered with straw. Real horses shook their manes and poked their heads over the white-washed fences around them. The waiters wore pink coats, white breeches, shiny black boots and white gloves. At another dance, I remember Meyer Davis telling the girls to take off their slippers, and when this was done, the lights were dimmed and the orchestra was silent except for the muted beat of drums—a wonderful Meyer Davis touch to Fred Astaire's "Dancing in the Dark."

Adapting ourselves to the stepmother situation from both angles, theirs and mine, was greatly enhanced by the many summers we spent at our camp in Maine. Despite the Wall Street crash and the fact that the country was facing the most difficult business crisis in its history, our new president offered us his New Deal, prohibition was repealed, and people began to hope everything would take a turn for the better. For us, year after year of those wonderful summers at Pretty Marsh wove together new family ties and lasting affections, partly because we all enjoyed the same things—sailing, climbing mountains, canoeing, digging clams. The girls had hosts of friends and we cherished visits from their Aunt Lou, my sister Eleanor, her husband Butler Windle, and pretty soon two sons-in-law, both of whom also revelled in camp life.

Yearly visits to South Carolina continued, sometimes with Shippen, sometimes with one of the girls. But drastic changes were taking place everywhere. Aunty Sinkler and Uncle Charlie died and there were no longer visits to Belvidere. For a time their daughter Anne, who had married Dr. W. Kershaw Fishburne and lived across country at Pinopolis,

29

ran the plantation as a working farm. Anne was twelve years older than I, and because she had moved away from Belvidere in 1910, I had not seen much of her for many years. It was wonderful to find a "new" loving cousin, and the many years of our increasingly close relationship from then on have been some of the happiest in my life. Like Shippen, she was one of those "special" people who are artists in their contacts with others. "Make opportunities for pleasure," she used to say. "Bring people together who enjoy each other." What a creed! Her house in tiny Pinopolis was a haven of hospitality.

Pinopolis is not to be confused with Pineville, but both were situated in the pine lands. Year after year in the Low Country, epidemics of fever took the lives of too many poeple, and it was the custom in summer on the plantations to move the whole family and house servants to Eutawville, Pinopolis or Pineville, and thus escape malaria. The cause of these fevers was then not known. All they did know was that in summer they *must* move to higher ground. It did not occur to them that the pinelands were drier, creating an environment in which the malarial mosquito could not thrive.

Pinopolis was about four miles from Monck's Corner, the latter once a place of commercial importance. Before the war, Santee planters took their crops to Monck's Corner, sold them for cash or goods in exchange, dined at one of the taverns, and returned to their plantations in the afternoon. Turpentine, tobacco, rice, cotton and indigo were taken to storehouses on the Santee Canal, or to barges at the ferry stations on the Cooper River and transported down river to Charleston.

In my day, Monck's Corner was a quaint community with a few country stores and service stations. There was a garden club founded by my cousin Anne, and the Berkeley County Library, with Anne as chairman of the board that created it. She was a skilled gardener, a brave horsewoman who enjoyed fox-hunting in the moonlight, and beautified the railroad station at Monck's Corner with a plot of flowers and shrubs which she personally tended. The long avenue into Pinopolis, lined with crêpe-myrtle and dogwood trees, was also due to Anne, and she and Kershaw together accumulated seven thousand dollars which provided the seed money that was the beginning of the Berkely County Hospital. There is now a little museum in Monck's Corner where the sword of our grandfather Julius Porcher now hangs, crossed with that of Wharton Sinkler's, his contemporary and friend, also a Confederate soldier. The two swords used to hang over the fireplace in the parlor at Belvidere, before that plantation was submerged under the waters of the Santee-Cooper Authority's hydro-electric enterprise, and it was Anne who had brought them to Monck's Corner. Our grandfather's sword has an ironic imprint on the blade: "United States of America."

The construction of the Santee-Cooper development, flooding the very heart of the South Carolina Low Country, turned many hearts against Mr. Roosevelt. A story is told that one of our country cousins arose every morning, turned her back on Lake Moultrie and cursed Mr. Roosevelt. Although poverty-stricken, she refused to touch the $32,000 the government paid her for her land, and the money remained in a bank in Columbia until her death. After the flooding stopped there were other stories about masses of animals seeking higher ground. Among them were countless numbers of the deadly water moccasin, and many country children died as a result. I knew the Pinopolis environment before and after the completion of the dams. It was an odd feeling to look out from the windows of a cousin's house and see sparkling water where there used to be cotton fields and woodlands. As for horseback riding, to trot down a sandy lane and find water lapping across it just around the corner was a distinct shock.

For those of us coming down from the north, reaching Pinopolis was much easier than reaching Belvidere. Monck's Corner was on the Atlantic Coast Line Railroad, and the Palmetto Limited from New York to Florida became as much loved as the Bar Harbor Express from Philadelphia to Bangor, Maine. How often over the years, how very often, I used to wake up in my lower berth, roll up the windowshade and find the train clackety-clacking through the open country, cotton fields and moss-draped cypress swamps. There was always the thrill that I was coming home, that here I was again in South Carolina with two or three weeks of Charleston activities, with Gus and Sam Stoney, DuBose and Josephine, and other handsome cousins to take me out to parties and picnics on Folly Island or Edisto. Even if there was no longer Belvidere to look forward to there was nearby Gyppy Plantation on the Cooper River which Anne's sister Emily and her husband Nicholas Roosevelt had bought. This was a wonderful place for a tilting tournament and barge parties floating down river past old rice fields where one could watch herons and egrets pass over the marshes in straggling flocks. As the train rattled on, familiar landmarks told me I'd better get dressed, for we were nearing Monck's Corner and soon the train slowed down, jaunted along for a bit, and finally drew up at the station, the sleeping cars always so far in the rear that the Pullman porter had to place a two-step on the tracks to help you down. Then, Anne's welcoming face and outstretched arms, followed by much kissing and hugging and carrying of bags as we stumbled along the railroad ties to the car. Everyone was

31

talking at once, Anne's voice delicious and soft, the southern accent warming my heart. At last, the white gates at Pinopolis, the rumble over the cattle-guard, the sandy drive through the tall yellow pines, past the garden, and Cheeka and Peach, the two "daughters of the house" standing at the top of the flaring brick steps on the terrace. More hugging and kissing and moving into the dining-room and Catherine coming out of the kitchen and another warm hug, and finally Kershaw rattling off grace and all of us sitting down to fruit, grits, scrambled eggs, bacon, sausages, corn bread, blood-pudding, cocoa, waffles and molasses.

On Shippen's first visit to Pinopolis he immobilized the entire breakfast table by pouring molasses over his hominy grits. The situation was saved by Cheeka, who shouted, "Hot dam! I bet it's good!"

My diaries at this time were divided into sections: writing, reading, politics, family, social life, and soon—Pearl Harbor. The political world had come to life under Roosevelt but things in Europe were not going well. Personally I was still determined to get on with my writing no matter what happened and stun the world with a great novel. I'd had some brushes with New York publishers and had an excellent agent, Mary Abbott with McIntosh and Otis. But it's a dreary life simply to be "promising."

However, I was getting into print here and there. Shippen and I had joined the Audubon Society's first bird trips in Florida, headed by Alexander Sprunt of Charleston. They were glorious experiences and I wrote half-a-dozen articles about them which appeared in *Bird Lore* under the name of Mary F.W. Lewis. Could any name be duller? There were hundreds of Mary Lewises all over the country—opera singers, poets, and writers. Then a check from the *American Magazine* for an article about being a stepmother that was published anonymously because I did not wish to embarrass my stepdaughters. Another check, from the *Ladies Home Journal* for "I wanted Applause" and, the translation into Japanese of one of my St. Nicholas stories helped to keep up my spirits.

I wish I had had enough sense to settle on a pen name and stick to it, but I didn't. Josephine Pinckney's whole name was Josephine Lyons Scott Pinckney and she dropped her middle names. My problem was that publishers above the Mason Dixon line insisted upon pronouncing Porcher *porch-er* and I could not stand the harshness of it.

Weezie was not long in following her sisters into matrimony and, after her marriage to Anderson Page, Shippen and I decided that we no longer needed the big house on Hartwell Lane. We were fortunate to find that 8018 Navajo Street was available, for this meant we could still bask in the congenial atmosphere of little old Navajo Street, and were but two back yards away from Sister Lou at 8030 Navajo. I loved the new house and, with the consent of George Woodward Jr.—then in charge of George Woodward, Inc.—we had a door built in the bay window of the dining room which opened on a flagstone terrace where we ate many of our meals in clement weather. I did not know when we moved into 8018 that my life was to take a sharp turn in other directions after the seventeen years I lived there. It was a lovable house, and, even when the time came, only the most unexpected circumstances could have lured me into leaving it.

I was still playing the piano, but gone were the days when I could practice three or four hours a day to keep up my "repertoire," which meant the number of pieces I could play without the music in front of me. The old-fashioned "parlor pianist" was out. Not only Victor records but the radio was in. Instead of counting on a person who could rattle off "The Vamp," "The Maple Leaf Rag," or "Three O'Clock in the Morning" so the crowd could dance or harmonize, all we had to do was switch the radio to a jazz station.

Shippen enjoyed my playing in the evenings at home and when the girls were young they had their favorites, too. But one of my most appreciative listeners was Aunt Carry Sinkler, my father's sister-in-law. Some years after her sister Aunt Lizzie married Eckley B. Coxe and came to live in Philadelphia, Aunt Carry also left Eutaw Plantation, South Carolina where she had grown up, and came to Philadelphia. During the winter she lived at 1604 Locust Street and in April moved out to "The Highlands," her beautiful estate in Fort Washington, Pennsylvania. During the summer she migrated still further north to Eastern Point, Gloucester, Massachusetts, returning to "The Highlands" for a short time in the fall before going back to Locust Street for the winter.

She was the most impressive grande dame I knew well—I can't quite say intimately, for she created a truly regal atmosphere. Her drawing-room on Locust Street with its concert grand piano, rose-colored silk panelled walls and gilded sconces challenged something deep within you, lifting you from commonplace affairs and turning you into an actor with a part to play. You felt uncomfortably out-of-place if you couldn't find something to contribute, not only drawing-room behavior—that was entendue—but a readiness, nay, an ability to play an enthusiastic part in the scenario she had set up. When her drawing-room was crowded, she kept herself off-stage by sitting partially behind a curtain separating the rear end of the room from a hall.

Woe to the invited guest who tried to slip away without making a formal farewell. To fall out of her favor was to risk being scratched off her list, and I for one was not going to take a chance of cutting myself off from her incredibly generous and efficient distribution of four, sometimes six seats in her box at the Friday afternoon concerts. Even at the last minute, if she had an unfilled seat, your telephone might ring and Anna Lee or one of the other maids would ask if you could use a ticket. Such was her prestige that you did not even need the ticket itself. All you had to do was to murmur to one of the aged ticket-takers behind their red velvet ropes at the Academy, "Miss Sinkler's box, if you please. Number twelve," and in you'd go.

More than once Aunt Carry wanted to give me an audience at one of her famous after-the-concert gatherings on a Friday afternoon. But I could not bring myself to do it. I can play well only to those who honestly want to listen, for like poetry classical music is a very private thing and one can tell instantly in an audience if there are people present who wished they weren't there. Sometimes I came and played to her alone. She would sit in a little room off the big one, and with the door wide open between us I would revel in touching the keys of that magnificent piano. One of her favorite pieces was Dubussy's "Girl with the Flaxen Hair."

Out in the country at "The Highlands" it was a different story. The piano (the same one) was in a drawing room half the size of the one in town, and after a dinner party when the guests moved to the library, or outside on the terrace, for coffee and liqueurs, nothing pleased me more than to be asked to "play something". This I did happily across the hall with the drawing room all to myself.

During her long règime the hallway inside The Highlands was famous for its hilarious wallpaper, the brainchild of a wildly imaginative French artist who had depicted Red Indians with feathered headbands dancing hand-in-hand around a bonfire with black slaves and white ladies and gentlemen dressed in Colonial wigs and flounces! In the background was a row of wigwams. On the opposite wall the artist had painted a glorious Niagara Falls-type of waterfall tumbling out of a clear sky next to what looked like the Natural Arch in Virginia!

Grand dame that she was, sometimes Aunt Carry's high-handed methods were—impish? It was only a three minute walk from her front door on Locust Street to the stage door of the Academy of Music, and frequently her protégés spent the night at 1604 between the Friday afternoon and Saturday night concerts. On more than one occasion she sent Stokowski's blood pressure soaring by detaining a violinist just a little too long at her house before his appearance on stage. As for informal moments, I have an especially endearing memory of a certain scene when one of her protégés, young Yehudi Menuhin, was her guest. After her tea party following the Friday afternoon concert came to an end and all the other guests were gone, Yehudi Menuhin, Aunt Carry and I sat together on the bottom of her carpeted stairs in the Locust Street house. Her ankle-length dress flowed gracefully about her, her mood congenial and relaxed. Anna Lee, the maid, had brought us three plates of chocolate ice cream and orange water ice "because there was so much left over after the party." I had lingered because I had wanted to ask Yehudi a question. "First," I said to him, "give me your left hand." He put down his plate of ice cream and did so and I touched each one of his fingertips, amazed that not one of them was calloused. Having had a mild experience with a guitar and the agony of pressing hard continuously against the wires, I was thankful that my concern was the smooth ivory of piano keys. He explained that a violinist's fingers go through the callous stage and somehow outgrow it to remain strong and sensitive.

Another of Aunt Carry's protégés was Walker Hancock, internationally known American sculptor who created the Pennsylvania Railroad war memorial which stands in Philadelphia's Thirtieth Street station. Walker always reminded me of DuBose Heyward, both being sensitive and compassionate artists in their own fields. The memorial was dedicated in honor of the thirteen hundred employees of the Pennsylvania Railroad who had lost their lives in the Second World War. He had meant the angel to be St. Michael, the traditional bearer of souls to heaven, and said that he had intended his "sketch models to represent the saint in armor, as is usual, but decided later to simplify the figure." One cannot gaze up at this angel of mercy holding in his arms a wounded soldier without being deeply moved by the power of its message.

I have so many memories of Aunt Carry, and, although she had once been a member of the now long extinct Democratic Women's Luncheon Club, it was difficult ever to visualize her standing in a line awaiting her turn at the voting booth, or associating herself with the merry-go-round ballyhoo of a political campaign, a situation in which I was to find myself in 1940.

A telephone call from Jack Kelly, Chairman of the Democrat City Committee, asking me to head up the Democratic Women's Campaign Committee for Roosevelt sent me into a tailspin. I knew nothing whatever about running a political campaign but Shippen encouraged me to accept the appointment. I did so and soon decided that what the power boys at city headquarters really wanted was Shippen's name and influence during the campaign. Before I knew it I was caught up in that dizzy merry-go-round, grasping frantically at every straw of help I could find.

With fear and trembling I attended my first assignment to preside over a rally at somebody's house on Sansom Street. The first person who stood up and challenged one of my suggestions threw me into confusion. I boggled the entire affair trying to please everyone and have been forever grateful to Crystal Bird Fausset, a committeewoman who, when I told her I had not wanted to make enemies, replied, "But you *have* to! You have to make the *correct* enemies!"

How fortunate we Democrats were in that campaign to have Mr. David Stern's *Philadelphia Record* on our side, holding its own against the three Republican papers, *The Inquirer*, *The Evening Bulletin* and *The Evening Ledger*. A reporter from *The Record*, Evelyn Shuler, was another great helper, very fair in reporting that Mrs. W. Plunkett Stewart, co-ordinator of the Wilkie women's group and I were "fighting fairly" and that a phenomenon of the campaign lay in the fact that "both women are scrupulously avoiding personalities and making generous concessions to the opposition."

One of the highlights of this campaign was our opponents' cry "Only paupers vote for Roosevelt!" Robert McCracken, a distinguished Philadelphia lawyer and a good friend of Shippen's uttered these words in a moment of enthusiasm during a campaign speech for Wilkie. Only three groups, he insisted, were going to vote for Roosevelt: paupers, those who never earned more than twelve thousand dollars a year, and the president's family.

The newspapers had a field day with this. It so happened that same day our Democratic campaign committee was holding an important luncheon of more than eight hundred people in the Bellevue Stratford ballroom. Our guest speaker was the glamorous Mrs. Anthony J. Drexel Biddle, wife of the United States ambassador to Poland. As chairman of the committee I was presiding and just about to introduce Mrs. Biddle when Jack Kelly made one of his dramatic entrances, dashed up behind the speakers' table, virtually pushed me aside and gleefully shouted "Hello—fellow paupers!" He then read a letter he had written to Bob McCracken which brought down the house and was printed in all the papers that evening. Before the day was over peddlers were on the street selling large buttons which said "I am a pauper for Roosevelt!" and the press enjoyed reporting that Mrs. Tony Biddle was heiress to eighty-five million dollars.

The most moving moment of the 1940 campaign occurred during

what we Democrats in Philadelphia called the "Martin, Barton and Fish" night when twenty thousand people crowded Convention Hall with seventy-five thousand outside unable to get in. There were two hundred people on the stage and I was one of them, seated in the second row behind a line of reporters and about ten feet from the podium. Spotlights swept their beams over the vast audience, the greatest crowd ever assembled there, as we waited for the President to appear, the great hall buzzing with highly charged expectations. All at once the huge curtain backstage slowly opened, creating a thirty-foot high isosceles triangle of light with Franklin Delano Roosevelt and two aides silhouetted at the bottom. As the trio moved forward toward the podium, the buzzing grew to a loud roar, and a chill ran up my spine when I saw on Roosevelt's face his look of tremendous self-confidence and mastery, not only of the occasion but of his infirmities. All you could think of was the strength of his will power, and as Jack Kelly stepped into the picture to introduce him in nine words, the aides vanished and there was Roosevelt standing alone at the podium, clutching it tensely with both hands to hold himself up, and beaming at an audience already in the palm of his hand. I don't recall his opening words but when he thrust his head forward, grinning, and began chanting slowly "Mar-tin," an avalanche of twenty-thousand half-laughing voices joined in with "Barton and Fish!" Each drawn-out syllable resounded through the hall, ending in pandemonium.

Jumping from the sublime to the ridiculous, I like to remember another episode during this campaign which occurred in Charleston when Josephine Pinckney outwitted Clare Booth Luce. Jo and Mr. Wilkie were friends and she knew he was to visit Mrs. Luce at her plantation, The Bluffs, on the Cooper river. So she wrote to Mrs. Luce inviting her and her guest to tea on a certain day. She received a rather cool note regretting that Mr. Wilkie was to arrive that very day and, alas, they would not be able to come. Jo knew exactly the day he was to arrive, drove out to the airport and met him when he got off the plane. The polite but baffled chauffeur from The Bluffs was quite helpless when Mr. Wilkie walked off with Josephine who drove him to her house in Charleston. Late for tea, but in person, Mrs. Luce appeared and shortly thereafter drove away with her kidnapped guest.

On November 6, 1940, the *Philadelphia Inquirer* used $2\frac{1}{4}$ inch-high letters for the headline, "Roosevelt Wins." Not to be outdone, the *Philadelphia Record* used the same $2\frac{1}{4}$ inch-high letters to scream out, "F.D.R. LANDSLIDE." Mr. Roosevelt was now facing his third term administration with plenty of problems ahead. The war in Europe was going badly for the Allies, and it looked as if we could not escape being drawn into it. Nor could we after December 7, 1941—Pearl Harbor, the Day of Infamy.

Our three sons-in-law enlisted: Anderson Page with the Air Force, Hunter Moss in the Marines, and Bill Townsend in the Navy. I too, got into uniform again, joining the Civil Defense. I took Air Raid Warning training at the Police College in town, and helped to open our Chestnut Hill headquarters at the Chestnut Hill Police Station and Fire House, on Highland Avenue. It was amusing to find myself one of the bosses in that childhood haunt of respect, where the firemen used to let us slide down the shiny brass pole from the second floor to street level. No more whinnying horses to rush out with engine, hook and ladder. Everything was modern now and motorized with elaborate instructions about dismantling bombs.

We were taught that dry sand falls 150 feet per second when used to control a fire; that a wet blanket over the left arm used as a shield could get you as near as five feet to fight a broken bomb. Under the heading "Home Protection Service" we were told how to instruct owners to keep blankets, sand and buckets on hand as well as an axe, a stirrup pump, a long handled shovel or scoop, flashlights, and a first aid kit. During a raid no one was to depend on spigot water, telephone, or electrical service. Most of all, when the alarm sounded people must *not* come outside to see what was going on, but should rush to the shelter where they had been assigned. It was all very exciting. We were even taught something about the difference between a thermal bomb, an ocean bomb and an oil-drum bomb. I am thankful to say that no bomb of any sort fell on Zone 42, and that my mastering of these instructions was never put to the test.

I soon found that my real contribution to the war effort was to become editor of a one-woman newspaper published by the Philadelphia Council of Defense. I called it "On Leave, What to Do and Where to Go in Philadelphia." The sheet, the size of a poster, was distributed every Friday, listing entertainment for servicemen: dances, dinners, and shows sponsored by what were to become thirty service clubs in the city. Nine hundred and fifty copies were posted around town in spots where they would reach groups of soldiers, sailors and airmen. Every ship docking at the Navy yard got a copy, and when French vessels were in port, a number were translated into French. Many of the gobs and GI's wanted to see "The Bell" in Independence Hall as well as to meet girls at the service clubs. To help me I had one secretary and a printer who worked at cost because he was a veteran. I enjoyed this work for three years, talking with the boys at the different service clubs, catching on to their lingo and using it on the newsheet. For example, "Pull the ripcord and drop into the dance at the USO Club Saturday night"; "Are your dates blind or blond? Find out at the Stage Door Canteen next Thursday night . . ."; "Wiggle your flippers and signal your pals to assemble on Tuesday at the YMCA . . ." Sports ranked first with the boys, even before girls; dances second; music third; museums and historical tours ("The Bell" excepted) fourth. Lectures were way down at the bottom of the list.

As time went on, "On Leave" began to become quite famous and we were naturally grateful when told by the Council of Defense that the national USO considered it the best paper of its kind in the country and that the New York branch was sending two hundred copies each week to camps overseas. After the war was over a discharged bluejacket wrote me a letter requesting a copy of the whole series because, he said, "Seeing it posted in my ship when in the Mediterranean, I felt kind of in touch with home."

Social life in Chestnut Hill was becoming confined to local neighbors. The last party of Main Line friends was on a May evening when they came in a station wagon, six of them, all the way over from Bryn Mawr to have dinner with us at 8018. Gasoline was rationed and a ban was soon to be put on pleasure driving. As they waved farewell, Bessie Evans called out, "Good-bye! See you after the Peace Treaty's been signed."

I was still signed up for FBI talks, stressing their program of "Security of War Information." It was hard to believe there were spies among us and that casual conversation on trains and in public places could possibly be dangerous, but we were urged never to discuss letters from our men overseas. I wrote in my diary for June 9, 1943:

North African campaign successful. Talk of Germans ready to use gas. Sickening. Our submarines seem to be getting defeated, I don't know how. Lots of Allied air raids on German industry. Every bit of it sickening. War movies are superb, horrible, thrilling, revealing. Noël Coward's movie, "In Which We Serve," marvelous. Air Force, bomber crew over the Pacific, North Atlantic patrol . . . a wonderful account of our merchant marine. Crash dive in color, submarine story hair-raisingly done. This is the only way I come in contact with violence—a horrible violence that all the young men in this generation are actually *living*, yet able to perform expertly under terrific situations, (the enemy as well). It makes me realize I am only on the outer fringe of this lunatic, mechanical adventure of modern warfare. For me there are thrushes singing and vegetables growing in our Victory gardens, and roses to cut in the morning and put on the dining-room table; and Yanny, my spaniel to stroke; a cocktail in the evening with Shippen and a comfortable bed, and church where people see their friends, and chocolate ice cream sodas after a hot day in town. The whole world is ripped open and I am only slightly inconvenienced. It's hard to get food but there's plenty of it even if variety is cut down. Meat is expensive but there's fish and fowl, plenty of fruit, vegetables, eggs and milk not yet rationed. The gas situation is tight and Chestnut Hill stores are delivering only three times a week. Even this scarcely inconveniences me for I can get about on my bicycle.

All kinds of peace groups were forming, blending, disappearing. There was the World Court, Foreign Affairs Council, the United Nations Council which, under John Nason, broke off from Union Now. I attended my first meeting of the Women's Committee of the Forum and we discussed a Forum Quiz for Philadelphia to alert new war workers to the existence of the Forum. Barbara Barnes Murdoch, feature writer in the *Evening Bulletin* had lots of good ideas.

Bill MacCoy, son of Shippen's law partner, W. Logan MacCoy, was killed on a flying field in Texas. His parents were on their way to see him get his wings, and, at St. Louis, where they changed trains they were informed of the tragedy. Logan must have telephoned the news to Shippen, for the next day he went over by bus to the MacCoy house in Overbrook to be with Bills' sisters. Bob Clothier, another friend of Logan's had lost his son a year earlier in a flying accident and was already with them. A few days later we all went to Bill MacCoy's funeral. Later, alone in my "studio," I played Cesar Franck's *Panus Angelicus* and my thoughts turned to the MacCoys and the funeral. I remembered how two cadets had folded the American flag that had been on the coffin as it was lowered into the ground, and how the undertaker had quickly laid flowers on it as if the coffin were too strong a sight for the beholders. But it was the poem about fliers read by the clergyman that was the last straw for me. We all felt that this sort of thing was just the beginning for us. In the face of it, life looked pretty clouded.

In July we managed to reach our camp in Maine. The Bar Harbour Express had folded up, so we took a train to Boston, spent the night in a hotel there, took a morning train to Ellsworth, Maine and a bus from there to Somesville on Mount Desert Island. Here Polly and Bill, who was on leave, met us in a rented Tin Lizzie, old and ancient with tires that could go no further than sixty miles without a blow-out—or at best a bulge of red inner tube sticking through the tire like a hernia. Polly dubbed it the "Upper Berth" because it rattled so.

A walk after dark in starlight down our drive through our woods, the Milky Way at an odd slant across the heavens, the glowing planets and the pure air, all lifted up my spirits and helped to put the depression of the past few weeks into proper perspective.

Chapter 4

1944–1951

BUT THE WAR WENT on and my brother tried to enlist, first in the Navy, then in the Army, but was turned down by both when medical examinations revealed tubercular scars on his lungs. This was a shock to us all, for there was no record of his having been ill. And then, on the fourth of April my Father died suddenly from a heart attack at his home on Navajo Street. He was in his eighty-seventh year.

Sorrow is a strange experience and lives on and on, sending down roots into the depths of our being, changing our entire outlook on life. Although my brother managed to join the Signal Corp, I was glad he could live at home with Mother. For a while I tried to come down to 7708 every morning and have breakfast with her. Each spring, even now, when the narcissus blooms and the snow-drops come out and the blue-bells and azaleas are in flower I can still share with my father his lasting love of them. I enjoyed editing his *Story of a Varied Career*, a collection of autobiographical fragments of his childhood in South Carolina and Virginia. At the age of four his father was killed in the Battle of Missionary Ridge, and his mother died when he was twelve. His Virginia family of Wickhams helped to send him to the Episcopal High School and through the University of Virginia.

Keeping sane in a world that continues to become increasingly technological requires beats and rests, moments of quiet in place of activity, space in exchange for crowdedness. And that summer of 1944 our camp on Mount Desert Island, Maine, provided just this. The simplicities of camp life amid the ever-changing rhythm of sun, fog, winds and tides build up a storehouse of energy that keeps you going even after you come home. There is nothing that lifts the spirit higher than watching an eagle overhead, soaring, circling above the sparkling bay, and the thought that white-winged crossbills have been singing in the tip-top of spruce trees from era to era, and that great blue herons have been fishing in quiet coves long before and after you are on the scene.

In such a lofty mood I returned to find Chestnut Hill and the Wissahickon doing their autumn act by turning poplar leaves into golden coins quivering against the sky. I remembered past autumns with field hockey, migrating warblers and a song we used to sing at Wissahickon Heights School:

> Fast fall the leaves now sere and yellow,
> > Great heaps are piled along the lane;
> Ripe are the apples, tart and mellow,
> > Gold are the fields of rippling grain.
> > > A faint warm haze
> > > Makes soft the blaze
> > > Of golden days.

Under pressure I again agreed to head the Democratic Women's Campaign for Roosevelt. I was not entirely in favor of a fourth term for any president. But who else was there for the Democrats? We were soon struggling in the throes of publicity, stunts, radio, loud speakers, rallies and meetings. Jerry Doyle, widely recognized as one of the country's outstanding cartoonists, and editorial cartoonist for *The Record*, opened our Women's Campaign Headquarters at 205 South 15th Street, where we set up a display of cartoons relevant to the current presidential campaign, showing Mr. Dewey loving the New Deal but hating the New Dealers. "Every time Dewey makes a speech," Jerry told us, smiling, "he gives me plenty of ammunition."

On September 27, our Women's Committee gave a luncheon for the vice-president, Mr. Henry A. Wallace. I had to preside with Mr. Wallace on my right and Senator Guffey on my left. I had always found the Senator difficult to talk to and turned to Mr. Wallace, plunging into soil conservation and contour ploughing, popular at that time. I spoke of Louis Bromfield's recent book on farming (he was hoping Roosevelt would make him his Secretary of Agriculture) as well as Mr. P. Allston Waring's contour ploughing experiment in Bucks County. Then I couldn't resist asking him if it were true that he had one day outrun his bodyguards on a street in New York, successfully losing himself in the crowd. Mr. Wallace admitted it was so—that he had been "desperate for a little privacy." I could sympathize with that and smiled a little to myself when he ordered a glass of milk instead of coffee, and dunked his roll in the milk.

That same night Philadelphia gave a roaring welcome to Mr. Roosevelt when he came to town to make a speech at Shibe Park. The newspapers printed a timetable of the tour, which included the Navy Yard, Camden Bridge Plaza, Cramp's Shipyard, parts of Germantown and the Wissahickon Drive. There had never been a bigger crowd at Shibe Park than on that night when we listened with delight to the President shattering many of Dewey's mis-statements. To some people's horror he drove around the park twice in an open touring car with Falla, the White House Scottie beside him, and many Secret Service men—a tempting target for gunshot or bomb. We had assassins in those days but not yet well-organized terrorist groups.

The night before election, Shippen and I listened over the radio to Dorothy Thompson's magnificent campaign speech, the finest speech from anyone during the whole campaign. Then we suffered through Mr. Dewey's remarks and I became more and more outraged to the point of scribbling angrily in my diary: "If Americans, foreign, native, rich or poor, women, poets, miners and farmers and stupid Philadelphians don't sock 'that little man on the wedding-cake' in the eye tomorrow, I'll eat Barbara Tyson's new mink coat publicly, outside Streeper's Drugstore."

I did not have to eat mink.

After a political campaign is over, especially if it's been a success, there is often a desire to keep the gang together. In Philadelphia and Pennsylvania in general there was a feeling among the Democratic women that we had to keep going somewhere. At the beginning of the campaign Susan B. Anthony 2nd, great-niece of the original Susan Anthony, dropped into Philadelphia out of a clear sky. She was a great help, full of ideas, energetic, and distinctly decorative. Together we drew up a year-round program for what we thought the Federation of Pennsylvania Democratic Women might do. To call attention to this program, state-wide, we organized a trip to the Electoral College scheduled to meet in Harrisburg at the Capitol on Dec. 18. Mrs. Emma Guffey Miller, National Committeewoman for Pennsylvania and sister of Senator Guffey, was head of the Federation, and was agreeable to the idea. But she was against any change in the way the Federation was being handled. We tried to point out that the purpose of our program was merely to make clearer a year-round schedule of activities which would bind us more tightly together. State Senator David Lawrence was in favor of our suggestions; so was congressman Francis J. Myers (candidate for U.S. Senator). Susan and I had no idea that we were to be double crossed in what we considered a cause worth the effort. We went cheerfully ahead and called on James Clark, the new Philadelphia Democratic City Chairman, Jack Kelly having resigned, and asked him

45

to provide us with two special cars to take the Philadelphia and Vicinity Delegation to Harrisburg on December 18. He politely arranged these matters for us, and a hundred and forty of us piled into the cars at Broad Street station. The train stopped at West Philadelphia where Mrs. Gifford Pinchot got on, and again at Paoli where Adele Saul and Gertrude Ely joined us. We arrived in Harrisburg and walked *en masse* up the middle of the streets to the Capitol and into the ornate Senate Chambers resplendent with Violet Oakley's wonderful murals.

The formalities of the Electoral College are slow and medieval. The Constitution provides that each state shall appoint a number of electors equal to that state's quota of senators and representatives who are to meet "on the first Monday after the second Tuesday in December to cast their ballots." The vote is then transmitted to the president of the Senate in Washington on January 6, who, in the presence of both houses of Congress, opens the certificates and counts the ballots from all the states. A president and vice-president are not officially elected until this little drama is enacted.

After two hours of droning resolutions from thirty-five individual electors, people began to get restless as well as hungry. Adele Saul, Gertrude Ely, Mrs. Pinchot, Connie Anderson (PAC), Susan and I left our seats and went into a corner of the chambers where we were joined by Mrs. Miller and Mrs. Ruth Horting, president and vice-president respectively of the Women's Federation. We felt a chill in the air. A women's meeting was to be held after a big luncheon at the Madrid Hotel ballroom, at which we expected to present our program. Rather abruptly Mrs Horting pulled out a book of the state committee rules which, in her words, superseded Roberts' Parliamentary Rules. Consequently our request for twenty minutes on the afternoon program had to be cancelled. She opened the book and showed us the words she had underlined: "No resolutions can be passed in the Commonwealth of Pennsylvania at a public meeting held by women." She went on to add, as if this settled everything, "But because so many ladies from Philadelphia have come today, we'll give you ten minutes."

We withdrew, shocked, skeptical and angry, and walked back to the Penn-Harris where I was told I'd have to make that ten minute talk. After a small drink and a bowl of pea soup, I disappeared behind a screen in the dining room and scribbled down a few ideas, then withdrew even more privately to the ladies' rest room. While in my cubicle I heard excited voices and the unmistakable crowing of Mrs. Emma Guffey Miller as she pronounced, referring obviously to Susan and me, "*Those* two young women from Philadelphia simply wanted to run the whole show! They're nothing but amateurs and green-horns!"

I felt myself burn with righteous indignation. "Of all the . . ." Then I let out my breath slowly and began to laugh.

"You *said* it, you old cackling hen! Green-horns? Amateurs? You said it, and I couldn't agree with you more!"

Politics or no politics, the war went on. Dora was hearing pretty regularly from Hunter, now in Saipan. Andy Page, desperately anxious to get to the front, was in Nebraska training others how to fly B-29's, and Bill Townsend had been shunted from the Pacific to the Atlantic and the Mediterranean. To save coal, Shippen and I put a caboose stove into our living-room and warmed ourselves with wood fires. It made a delicious heat and we decided to give a "Caboose Party" on New Year's Eve. Those present were near neighbors: Bonnie and Monk Wintersteen, Cooper and Martha Smith, Natalie and Charlie Kinsolving, Ted and Alice Madeira, Gardner and Ella Aspinwall, Sydney and Margaret Martin, Herbert and Mary Goodrich, Eddie and Katherine Clay and George and Jean Trowbridge. Both Cooper Smith and Monk had to leave early for Coast Guard duty. After the martinis, we had naturally, for a caboose party, a large pot of Irish stew with rolls, celery, olives, nuts, mince pie and coffee. Someone proposed a toast: "With confidence and trust in the New Year, with courage and strength from our friends." At midnight we sang "Auld Lang Syne" and "The Star Spangled Banner"—a good way to welcome in the frightening year of 1945.

On Thursday, April 12, while sitting for his portrait at Warm Springs, Georgia, Franklin Delano Roosevelt had a stroke and a few hours later was dead—mercifully quick. The mourning across the country was staggering. The radio stations deleted all commercials for forty-eight hours, the whole time given over to tributes by famous people and to classical music. I had a sense of personal loss for weeks. My nights were troubled with tragic dreams and a queer sense of doom and dislocation. But the government did not fall apart, nor did we. The following day Shippen and I went downtown to Old Christ Church for the memorial service where we saw many, many friends. Afterwards I met Emily Myers who said she was avoiding some of her friends because she was behaving so badly. "When you have loved someone so much," she said, "and others don't understand, you just have to keep quiet." A day or two later I ran into Bessie Evans along Peacock Alley at the Bellevue. We rushed into each other's arms and wept.

The San Francisco Conference was not cancelled. Stalin was sending over Molotov, his top man, and the war was almost over in Germany. But General Eisenhower said there would be no V.E. Day announcement until the last pocket of resistance in Germany was over. Focus was now centered on Okinawa near Japan. We didn't know where Hunter Moss was, for there was no word that his second Marine joint assault force was involved in that desperate battle. It was hard, and sickening for Dora.

"On Leave" was still being published, and my diary recorded that we were having an amazingly early spring—four weeks ahead of schedule. Everyone began planting their victory gardens and, with Polly's help, we had a small vegetable patch in our front yard at 8018 Navajo Street. I was endlessly fascinated that our suburban front and back yards of Chestnut Hill could produce delicious fresh carrots, peas, string beans, celery, radishes and lettuce. Around the corner on Hartwell Lane M.T. Cooke grew the finest and most perfect Boston lettuce. As for the spring flowers, everything was blooming at once—wistaria, dogwoods, azaleas, viburnam, lilies-of-the-valley and lilacs.

Perhaps because it was spring I felt a little more cheerful about my writing, cheerful in the sense that I could remember DuBose Heyward saying, "But you keep on trying." I also recalled what Hervey Allen had written to me ". . . the thing to do with publishers is to have a peacock feather and use it like a club!" Trying to think proudly of my work, I did realize that certain personalities in my constant attempts at writing a best seller seemed to stay alive in my mind despite their changed names in each new manuscript. In fact, they began to challenge me. What I needed was a structure, a plot, and tricky scenes to pull it all together. There they were, off-stage, all those characters ready at a moment's notice to do my talking for me. I knew the background would be Philadelphia, for I'd had it drummed into me that one must write about what was familiar. But Philadelphia has a unique personality. The Schuylkill River plays a strong part in dividing "Philadelphians" between the Main Line and the Chestnut Hill-Penllyn-Springhouse-Jenkintown contingent. A great number who live outside the city limits carry on their business and professional lives within those limits but vote elsewhere. Socially they are all mixed up together through the Philadelphia Orchestra, and Philadelphia theatres, museums, clubs, and charitable organizations.

What, I asked myself, are most people truly interested in? I scoured the newspaper headlines: violence, power, babies, dogs, bad news, money. I knew I couldn't write a 70,000 word novel about babies or dogs; nor violence; nor sexy stuff. I knew nothing about power, but what about money? One thing I did know was this: No matter how wealthy some of my friends were, there were times when they shocked me by being stingy and downright mean. It occurred to me that I might have a little fun with this. Mischievous anecdotes passed through my mind. Being married to a lawyer, I thought wills might help me out, and I went to the rare book department of the Free Library on Logan Circle and found a book called *Unusual and Eccentric Wills*. For over an hour I sat at a table, pad and pencil in hand. Most wills are too complicated for normal, everyday people to understand, but I found a humdinger. At last a marvelous opportunity for my impatient off-stage characters!

Briefly, a rich Viennese gentleman in 1689, hating and hated by his family, bequeathed, let us say, $25,000 apiece to nine relatives and one old friend, with the understanding that no one should attend his funeral. If anyone did so he'd lose his bequest. The remainder of his estate was to go to charity. Of course there was a codicil to be read only after the funeral, which provided that if anyone out of affection or respect *did* appear at the graveside, that person would inherit his entire estate.

I warmed to the task. Everything devilish in me came to the fore. Everything catty, snobbish, sneering, and snickering began to simmer. I called my book *Device and Desire*, taken from the General Confession in our Protestant Episcopal Book of Common Prayer: "We have followed too much the devices and desires of our own hearts." I added a subtitle: *A Novel of Bad Manners* and set to work. What fun it was! All my frustrations over the years, my fury with stupid editors and publishers who refused to publish my work, my hours of despair in my studio along the Cresheim Creek, my envies of other people's success, headlines, and appearances on best seller lists, all were tossed into a big pot, which I stirred like an old witch, spicing it with family anecdotes not only from my own family but from others which I began to collect.

My enthusiasm carried me into the summer and to our camp in Maine where I built a little get-away cabin in the upper woods of our property. Here my characters began to take over with a vengeance and I found out that I was actually writing a satire on greed, and that the motive behind each character was to get the better of someone else, by hook or by crook. I also enjoyed setting the scene in a diabolically hot spell during one of Chestnut Hill's hottest summers, culminating in a fierce thunderstorm on the day of the funeral.

With everything spinning along in high gear, plus our summer activities of sailing, canoeing, and eating crab and lobster with our summer friends, we were all shaken out of our private affairs through the report of the first atomic bomb to be used in warfare—on August 6, at Hiroshima. Three days later another was dropped on the seaport of Nagasaki. On August 14, President Truman announced that Japan had surrendered unconditionally; and on September 2, on the U.S. battleship *Missouri* in Tokyo Bay, General MacArthur received the formal surrender from Japan. World War II was over, and in our immediate family there was profound gratitude that all three of the sons-in-law would soon be on their way home.

In a mild fashion I assisted in the fall elections—a "Row Office" affair. It was impossible to arouse public interest. Jim Clarke, a good-looking but rather colorless personality, resigned as Democratic city chairman and it was some time before Mike Bradley took over. Everyone down there at Democratic headquarters in the Bellevue Annex seemed to be asleep.

In the spring of 1946 my brother was taken ill with tuberculosis. Eleanor came over from West Chester each week to spend a night with Mother. Dr. Cooper, the tuberculosis specialist, told us that St. J. had only a few weeks to live, and he was taken from 7708 to All Saints Hospital on Stenton Avenue. Dr. Rex wanted to drive him there himself, and I went up first to be waiting in the room assigned to him. I waited a long time, and when they finally arrived I said to Dr. Rex, "Why were you so long?" "Because I knew he would never see another spring and we drove around the neighborhood; it is so beautiful now."

I had several long talks with my brother. He knew he was dying, but his rapid decline was shocking. He said he'd never wanted to live as long as Father had, and only regretted that he had not accomplished more. I spoke of his inventions for the Signal Corps, and he replied, "Yes, that's the job that killed me but this is not a bad way to die." His was a scientific mind, ahead of its time, and I often think of how much he would have enjoyed the computers of today. I asked if he were suffering and he shook his head, nor was he frightened. "You're in such a high fever all the time you're living in a different world, and starvation makes strange images and everything is unreal." He was tremendously interested in what was happening to him, and complained that everything was mysterious and nothing explained. I told him that I loved him and he said he knew that. Two days before he died I sat with him again but he was too weak to speak clearly. When I reached the door to leave I paused and turned my head. He smiled feebly and managed to raise his arm, then whispered, "Good-bye." He died on June 3, 1946, four days before his forty-fourth birthday.

Weeks followed in which I had strange thoughts about the religion in which I had been brought up. There was a rigidity about ecclesiastical matters that distressed me. I had considered myself a good enough Episcopalian and now wondered if I was not actually a heretic. But I could not possibly envision a neighborhood without its churches. I tried and tried to pull myself together and accept the fact that the powers that had our destinies in hand must be working out something for St. J, and there was nothing I could do about him but let him go. I even went through a period when I decided to stop writing. Ambition appeared as the supreme vanity, and success, so-called, naught but a tinkling cymbal.

That autumn, as the chairman of the Events Committee of the United Nations Council, I helped to stage an atom bomb show at the Academy of Music. The UNC, in cooperation with the Forum, the Philadelphia Association of Scientists, and Philip Regan Associates, undertook to project pictures of atom bombs in test actions onto a huge screen. Our speakers were David Lilienthal of the TVA and Thomas Finletter, with over ninety people on the stage. Mr. Lilienthal was scheduled to make a fifteen minute talk on the radio and it was tricky trying to fit everyone into this tight program—including Miss Fanny Wister. Each speaker was given the exact number of minutes on stage and because we knew that Miss Fanny was apt to linger over her remarks, we gave her four minutes but scheduled her for twelve! Violet Oakley's paintings were being exhibited in the Academy lobby, and Miss Fanny, a member of the Academy of Music Board, wanted to make sure that everyone present would take the time to look at them. The whole affair went off like clock-work, although we did have a tiny bit of a problem luring Miss Fanny back to her chair.

Keeping busy helped to put me in a more balanced emotional level, and I actually got back to *Device and Desire*. Regardless of vanity and peacock's feathers, I'd started something and was determined to finish it. From the start the book had fallen neatly into five parts: The Will, the Beneficiaries, the Funeral, the Codicil, and the Settlement. I had only part five to complete and my characters cheered me up. They actually made me laugh. What a sly little "Chippy Off the Old Block"—(headline of a review in the Los Angeles newspaper later on) my Ellen Purdon, young and beautiful, had turned out to be! What fun to have her spoken of as "outsmarting a flock of Philadelphia lawyers." She kept putting me into a splendid mood of mockery, disdain and mischief. At last the final words were written, the typed sheets lovingly packed up and sent to Mary Abbott in New York. And after that, as every author knows, you look at yourself helplessly in the mirror and ask "What now?" You are devastated, empty, useless. Books are like children. Once out of the hands of the parent-author they live lives of their own and, as I knew only too well, may die unborn.

Device and Desire didn't. Some weeks ahead, perhaps months, a telephone call from Starr Cornelius of the Lippincott editorial staff set me quivering. Would I have lunch with her at the Barclay on such and such a day? I did. She had brought my manuscript with her and I felt weak. Starr became a long-time friend indeed. She handled me superbly. Oh yes, they were interested but—I felt weaker—Ellen Purdon had to have a boy friend.

"Why?" I countered. "The book's a will story."

"She has to have a boy friend. There *has* to be a romance."

So, manuscript in hand, it was back to the drawing-board as it were, where I concocted a young lawyer, son of the Purdon family attorney and went through the whole 72,000 words tucking in here and there scenes for the new character who proved to be what today we would call just another self-seeking ambitious young Yuppie. Indeed he fitted in very well. But I couldn't help wondering, Would I pull it off? Or was this just another lame duck destined for oblivion?

Not a bit of it. Louise, my youngest stepdaughter, was with me that morning at 8018 Navajo Street when the telephone rang and the familiar voice of Starr Cornelius said, "I have news for you." Long pause.

"You mean I can get excited?" My voice shook.

"Yes. The contract for *Device and Desire* is in the mail. Congratulations. We are all very pleased."

I don't recall what else was said, but after hanging up Louise and I were in a rapturous embrace and began dancing around the room with joy. Naturally my whole attitude toward writing, my "career", myself, my family, my future, were highly charged with a powerful injection of confidence.

I thought at once of the second novel I was writing called *The Petrified Gesture*—a story utterly different from *Device and Desire*. I had hated having to resort to broad-casting bad news, the nasty, the mean, the snobbish and the greedy in order to entrap a publisher's interest. It went against all my early ambitions to seek out wherever I could find them—beauty, rhythm, and harmony. I was a poet and a musician as well as an impatient and ambitious novelist. Would I have to choose between them? I realized that publishers adored authors on whom they could slap labels—authors who could turn out a new Gothic, a new thriller, a new horror story, a new whodunit, or create unforgettable detective personalities year after year. Could I do that? Maybe, but I wasn't sure.

I disliked labels: they are too confining. We'd first have to see how *Device and Desire* was received. In the meantime, I was glad to be rid of greed and satire, and intended to keep on exploring the possibilities of *The Petrified Gesture*.

A long time before I had written a short story about a woman who committed a perfect suicide, but it was returned twice by magazine editors who said, "We do not publish suicide stories." I recalled a particular scene in that story which I thought I might use in the new book. The novel revolved around a woman, Camille Sharswood, who tried to drive out passion with gratitude. Not yet forty, her doctors had given her little time to live. She went back to the security of her home in Charleston and fell in love with a cousin, Louis Gironde, a well-known ornithologist. In the time left to her she wanted to show her gratitude, and on her return to Philadelphia she tried to turn over the estate of her deceased husband, a Philadelphia banker, to the Academy of Natural Sciences, with the proviso that Gironde be the director.

I listened to a great deal of music during the writing of this book— Cesar Franck, Tchaikowski, Debussy, Sibelius, Grieg, Rachmaninoff. No Wagner, no mathematical Bach, just the romantic classics. I steeped myself in harmony and beauty. Also, a trip to Charleston, with my friend Bonnie Wintersteen, enriched my love of that city and all that it meant to me. Bonnie had never been there before, and after a few ambles around The Battery, Tradd, and Church Streets, she exclaimed, "I had no idea that the United States had such a beautiful city as this!" With her knowledge of architecture and art, and her position as president of the Philadelphia Art Museum her appreciation was a delight. She had other interests as well, including golf; she broke the woman's record at the Charleston Country Club, becoming famous overnight!

For a long time now I had made it a habit when visiting Charleston with or without Shippen of giving a cocktail party the night of our arrival at the Fort Sumpter Hotel on The Battery. Cousinly hospitality was difficult to repay, for certain special relatives rarely came to Philadelphia. The trick was to *pre*-pay in this manner. This year there was balmy, heavenly weather, and I could introduce Bonnie at the cocktail party to fifteen or twenty of my kin. We were instantly caught up in a social whirl and the whole week turned out to be one of those episodes which belong to that wonderful period when "our hearts were young and gay." There is nothing like those crafty southern men who know how to make any woman they think worthwhile noticing feel like a "belle" and someone quite out of the ordinary. My cousin Louisa Popham's husband Bill, a former naval golf champion, now a retired admiral, set Bonnie up for more games with captains and admirals which resulted in an invitation to cocktails on board a destroyer in the harbor. As if the frenzied pace of our social life was not enough, we were swept into the wedding of a cousin's favorite daughter which included magnificent lunch parties featuring shrimp pies, corn breads, sweet potato puddings and she-crab soup. All of Charleston was agog about the wedding, and the bride's uncle, Sam Stoney, summed it up when he said, with a gleam in his eye, "There has been no wedding like it since the wedding of Galilee."

Perhaps what Bonnie and I enjoyed most was our visit to Anne and Kershaw Fishburne at Pinopolis. Once inside their gateway we were thrilled to see camellias in bloom—this was January—and a few narcissus coming out. To add a finishing touch to our ecstatic South Carolina visit was the theatrical, after-dark, boarding of the northbound Palmetto Limited at the Monck's Corner station. In those days if there were passengers who wished to get off or on at Monck's Corner, convenient to several plantations thereabouts, even the big trains would stop. The procedure was distinctly "back-country." There we were, Bonnie and I and our "seeing-off" party standing on the dismal small platform. When we heard the approaching train a long way off, Anne walked to the naked electric bulb on a pole, pulled a string, and the light went on. The approaching monster replied with a long "ah-woo-woo-ah", cast its dazzling headlights which lit up the whole countryside and began to grow bigger and bigger. We began to feel as small as insects and finally the train came to a jangling stop, the locomotive panting and blowing off steam and leaving the sleeping cars (as usual) nowhere near the platform. So we had to traipse with our bags and baggage down the cross-ties to be helped aboard by the Pullman porter and his two-step.

Back at home I found it immensely comforting and convenient to be involved with a home-town book publisher. The Lippincott people sent me a schedule of what was going to happen when, and this glimpse of the art of book-making and publishing set a high standard in my mind equaled only years later in my experience with Collins of London. One of the first things that went into action was a fascinating correspondence with Stanley Chambers, the Lippincott publicity manager. What a joy to be told that "in order to promote your book most effectively we must have up-to-date information about both you and the book." What a pleasure it was to send him a list of friends to whom advanced copies could be read, hoping for favorable quotes for the jacket cover and newspaper advertisements. They all came across magnificently—Hervey

Allen, Henry Seidel Canby, Struthers Burt, Emily Kimbrough, Josephine Pinckney. However, due to certain conservative Lippincott policies, they only used part of Hervey's delicious remarks, leaving out what I liked best when he called the book "more witchy than bitchy, but very witchybitchy." How relaxing and enchanting to hear about a "spring sales conference which will present your book and others for the remainder of the year." All of this was routine I know, but ambrosia to me. After half a century, at least one early ambition was being fulfilled: the reaching out and finding people beyond the circle of family and friends who were compatible.

I first saw the unbound pages of the book at our camp in Maine. The post mistress at the Mount Desert Post Office in Somesville called up at half-past four one day and said the package I'd been looking for from J.B. Lippincott had arrived and if I wanted it, to come in and get it before five o'clock. Ten minutes earlier I had put a cheese soufflé into the oven which would require thirty more minutes of cooking. The post office was fifteen minutes away. Could I risk it? I rushed out to the car, flew into Somesville, grabbed the package and speeded back to camp telling myself, "If the cheese soufflé comes out all right the book will be a success!" I opened the oven door. Perfect! I turned off the oven, took out the soufflé, tore into the package and there it was—a stitched copy of *Device and Desire*, title page, everything! This required a celebration. Shippen had gone down to Philadelphia a week before but the Peppers were still around. Beside myself with joy I covered the soufflé lightly, grabbed a flashlight, tucked the book under my arm and scrambled up through the woods to the Pepper camp. Lalite and Perry were just as excited as I was. We drank toasts to the book, to Shippen, the soufflé, the Lippincotts and ourselves, then ate the soufflé. The crowning touch was Lalite's telling me she once had "taken up book-binding" and that if she could remember how to do it she'd bind this one!

She was as good as her word. Just before Christmas, she presented me with her leather-bound copy in soft olive-green calf with gold lettering, the end papers in a lovely design of olive and Chinese red. It was beautiful, all done by hand which made the book look like a masterpiece. In fact, when Moncure Biddle, a member of the Board of the Free Library saw it he said to me, "Of course you'll give this to the library."

"Why?" I demanded.

"Because it belongs in our rare book department. It was written by a Philadelphian, bound by a Philadelphian, and published by a Philadelphian."

So that was that, and there the beautiful little thing remains to this day.

Device and Desire was a success. It appeared on the best seller list for a few weeks; the *Evening Bulletin* condensed it into its "Book of the Week"; Joe Lippincott, Sr. wrote me, "You're famous"; and the book went into a second printing.

Besides autographing parties and appearances at women's clubs, *The Inquirer's* Book and Author Luncheon put me on schedule with Margaret Widdemer, Cleveland Amory and Dr. Norman Vincent Peale. The report in the paper the next day was a rather bleak description of the occasion. Two of their three columns were given to Dr. Peale (a weekly contributor to the paper's Sunday Magazine) while the rest of us were squeezed into one. They spoke briefly of Cleveland Amory's *Proper Bostonians*, adding that he was writing a new book about a man who wrote a book. As for Margaret Widdemer and me, we were given about two sentences apiece. "Most of today's novels are not written by regular people," she had declared, not explaining what she meant by "regular." And I was quoted as having said "there's nothing like the expectancy of money to bring out people's characters."

Then there was a pride-satisfying luncheon at Sardi's Restaurant in New York. I was supposed to speak over the radio to newspaper reporters from other cities. On the leather banquette beside me was a very good-looking movie actor (his name forgotten, poor dear) who was going through the same promotions stunt that I was. The only result of this anyway was a photograph of me in *Promenade Magazine*, a New York city inter-hotel publication. A page was given to "six personalities who are getting 1950 off to a good start." I was spoken of with kind words, ending "Her profile is Bergmanesque, her sports—golf and shooting rapids in a kayak."

Of course, in Charleston and Pinopolis I was treated with sincere affection and plenty of Huguenot over-dramatization, one of their delightful specialties. In *Judy Jennings' Note-book*, she wrote:

> Charleston, which is self-styled America's most historic city and also is known as the City of Gates and Doorways, has through inter-marriages many connections with Philadelphia. Well known to both cities are such names as Sinkler, Stoney, Gadsden, Hastie. Fact is Mrs. Shippen Lewis (the former Mary Porcher) has oodles of connections with this southern community and has just returned from a gay visit to Charleston. The story is going the rounds when she went there to autograph her book *Device and Desire* she was almost embarrassed by the hospitality afforded her by the Charleston press. She met an eminent Charles-

ton lawyer in mid-town one mid-morning and after appropriate greet-
ings he bowed with characteristic courtliness and said, "My
congratulations not only on your book but on your publicity. When
Senator Byrd was in our midst the press gave him six inches. You, my
child, acquired six columns!"

My favorite review headlines were, "Chippy off the old block wins
reward for disobedience." "Satire in Acid and Old Lace"; "One of the
more surgically adept jobs of hide removal I've seen in years." And my
very, very favorite review appeared in *The Legal Intelligencer*—the official
newspaper for the publication of all legal notices in Philadelphia County.
The review starts out by saying that the paper did not normally review
novels and that the cast of characters were only third and fourth generations
of Philadelphians, but that they did represent a true segment of
Philadelphia. They were treated "in a gently satirical fashion suggestive
of that which J.P. Marquand dealt with the Apleys of Boston." A
reference to my having absorbed "a not inconsiderable knowledge of the
law, possibly from her distinguished husband Shippen Lewis" is to put
it mildly. At every turn of a legal situation or conversation, all I had to
do was to ask Shippen for the correct lingo and analysis of the situation.
However, for the court scene, I did go into the Orphans' Court in City
Hall and watch certain proceedings at first hand.

By this time I was well into *The Petrified Gesture*. I wrote it in a year's
time and that summer in Pretty Marsh I often took my portfolio and
went off in my kayak to write in lonely coves among the islands. It is
hard to communicate to your family the intense pressure under which
you write when the work is going well. Your characters are far more
real, important and absorbing than the flesh and blood people around
you, which, to say the least, is insulting. You have to learn to be
ruthless, even if it makes you feel like a worm when you steal the time
to do what your heart is set on. The best way, I finally discovered, was
to remain out of sight.

On one occasion that summer when the whole harbor and every camp
around it was aquiver over the impending arrival of the Northeast Harbor
Yacht Club cruise—a flotilla of two hundred sloops, schooners, yachts
and launches ending their races and anchoring for the night along our
quiet shores—I took to my kayak heading for a cove on Bartlett's Island
where I was sure to be alone. When I came around the point I found
to my disgust that a ketch was already ahead of me, the "Emily Marshall"
with its distinguished owner Samuel Eliot Morison on board. Like me
he had run for cover against the incoming fleet. He called to me over
the side and said he was finishing the last chapter of his naval history

The Coral Sea and after a few more polite remarks we promised to leave each other alone.

That autumn I finished *The Petrified Gesture*, so I thought, and sent it into the friendly atmosphere of the Lippincott publishing house. In due time George Stevens himself, a former member of The Algonquin Round Table, telephoned to me and said, "It's perfect." But not quite. He had a suggestion to make. They didn't want me to write another will story, why, I never found out. The suggestion was to turn the will into an endowment, and Starr Cornelius, bless her heart, would discuss it with me over another of those luncheons at the Barclay.

On the whole, the writing of *The Petrified Gesture* had many moments of delight. I had been careful to make the rounds in South Carolina, squeezing information out of everyone who might be of help. Herbert Ravenel Sass, a bird expert among other things, and known as "Hobo," wrote to me frantically: "I started to send you a telegram but decided that would be too spectacular. No! the least bittern *never* flies with the other herons! If you have sent a least bittern into the air with those other high-flying herons the late William Bartram, your honored fellow-citizen, will turn over in his grave."

Sam Stoney told me what it was really like in Charleston at the end of the summer. "Oleanders would still be in—they make Charleston more flowery than at any other time. Jo Pink had her say about drains in *Three O'Clock Dinner*, but you can always imagine a salty smell from the rivers coming in with the swing of the winds towards evening. Sometimes the harbor is full of classes of small boats all racing over varied courses at the same time. You eat cold things—lobster, crabs, salads, shrimp. And people don't walk out in the sun if they don't have to."

Anne Fishburne was voluble about mocking-birds. "They out-sing nightingales, and light sleepers get angry with them for some sing *all night!*" Her daughter, Emily Whaley, described Charleston gardens at summer's end, dilapidated and still, "as if a bad fairy had put a spell over them."

At one point I needed advice of a scientific nature and went to the bird department of the Philadelphia Academy of Natural Sciences to ask for help. A Mr. James Bond, curator of birds, was on hand and helped me out. I had met him once before when Alex Sprunt of Charleston had come to the Academy to make an address, and had spent the night with us at 8018. Until then I had only known him through the fascinating introduction he had written for his first book *Birds of the West Indies*. A certain paragraph struck me with the thought that, for heaven's sake, here was a museum man who actually sounded like a human being, not the typical musty, crusty little scientist tucked off in a dusty corner of the Academy, looking up at you from his shells, birds, or fossils with crooked spectacles sliding down his nose. I quote from that paragraph:

> At an elevation of over six thousand feet on Morne La Selle in Haiti, one can live luxuriously on wild strawberries and the best artichokes in the world, and often be able to buy cigarettes and bread brought up from Port au Prince by native women—and all this in the territory of the rare White-winged Crossbill and La Selle Thrush.

It was the mixture of wild strawberries and White-winged Crossbills which delighted me.

The Petrified Gesture did not go into a second printing. Every book has a history of its own. But it got some splendid reviews and many gratifying letters. I was not familiar with Henry James's *The Wings of a Dove*, and when I named my heroine Camille I was thinking entirely of the South Carolina camellias. The *Chicago Tribune*'s headline "It's Not Quite Henry James, But It's Good" gave me a bit of a shock, but it was my own fault for having my Camille compared to Mr. James's. Many authors rise above reading their reviews—or pretend to—with a kind of superiority which soothes the pain of a bad review. To my mind you can learn from the reviews what you've done well and where your weak points are. Only one review, in the *New York Times Book Review* upset me, for I felt the reviewer wanted to damn the whole story—why, of course, I couldn't figure out. She insisted that the author's "over-all philosophy was expressed via her characters in murky beatitudes and petrified gestures of despair." All I could think of was another of DuBose Heyward's remarks that it was hard to find "anyone in New York who understood what you are trying to say." So much for Charleston versus New York!

Quite naturally I dwelt especially on three letters, one from Struthers Burt, another from Henry Seidel Canby, and quite a correspondence with Curtis Bok. Struthers wrote:

> In all candor your first chapter made me a little afraid. I thought your book was going to be too perfervid, but once I got past that I wasn't a bit afraid. Knowing the Wissahickon and Charleston so well I got the full flavor of your subtle and accurate differentiations and loved your lovely descriptions. Once more my congratulations.

Mr. Canby's letter is one of my treasures:

> I am always long behind in my reading for pleasure. Now I have read *The Petrified Gesture* well and carefully and with much appreciation, as

I happen to know the Wissahickon as well as Charleston. Your Camille it seems to me is your great success and your Charleston goes deeply with me as background. There is much to my taste and a little too much of literary romanticism in your Gironde, as if Sam Stoney had drunk wild liquors and told himself a story. But Camille is the substance of the characters of the most notable novels. I shall read anything you ever write.

With such interest and encouragement from men like these, I managed to survive Curtis Bok's tirade. The two books, one following the other so closely stirred him up. He was horrified with *Device and Desire*. He said all the characters emerged as "humanized bad manners" rather than "bad-mannered humans." He said they were merely types with no "redeeming qualities, hence the book was neither a good novel nor a good case history." He pointed out "lost chances" in the plot and why not? Wasn't he the president judge of the Court of Common Pleas No. 6 in City Hall? His ambition in life was to see that justice is done and he didn't like it a bit when Ellen, a "chippy off the old block" outsmarted a whole flock of Philadelphia lawyers!

I was deeply touched that he took so much interest in the book and quickly wrote back why I had written it, namely that bad news made the headlines, that I was desperately trying to get my toe in the door with a published novel, and finally did so by cooking up a whole stew of bad people, bad actions, and bad news.

Curtis wrote back "So *that's* it!" and after reading *The Petrified Gesture* he wrote "That's much, much better," and that he was glad I'd got my toe in the door. His parting words were, "Well, what comes next?"

CHAPTER 5

1951–1952

IN THE WAKE OF World War II a strange uneasiness invaded the general chaos that follows all wars. Some saw this with an indifferent relief, others with concern, as if a rare species was being relegated to the endangered list. But it was increasingly clear that the time had come for "ladies" and "gentlemen" to walk off the stage. In Philadelphia, as well as in Boston, Baltimore, Richmond and surely in New Orleans and Charleston, engraved invitations were on the way out and dèbutante receptions and balls were the exception rather than the rule. In Philadelphia the *Bulletin*'s "Evening Chat" began to report as social occasions large money-raising gatherings for the benefit of museums, hospitals and other good works. These were held in the ballrooms of the Bellevue, the Ritz and the Warwick and were composed of such a variety of Philadelphians that they fulfilled the American dream of ourselves as the world's greatest "melting-pot."

Private life, too, was having its problems. Women were invading man's sacrosanct worlds of business and politics, even their clubs. Brave women attempted to bring up their children, run a home and at the same time have a job. Children's nurses were replaced by babysitters; cooks by TV dinners and "fast foods." Sinks were piled with unwashed dishes, pots and pans. Beds weren't made and households were in revolting disarray. Sometimes I couldn't help smiling with sympathy at some young husbands who, used to trained maids and butlers suddenly, through love and marriage, found themselves in the inexpert hands of the girls of their dreams.

I knew that others were feeling the same general shaking up of their familiar environment and I was one of those who was concerned. Among them was E. Digby Baltzell, one of our country's leading experts in social history who was beginning to chronicle upper class life in

61

Philadelphia, analyzing post-war changes with scientific objectivity. He called those changes "other direction trends"—"other" implying moving away from the traditional into "democratic camaraderie." He spoke of the new "corporate feudalism in America" himself wondering if this might prove to be "more socially stultifying than the traditional family and class hierarchies of the past."

This was exactly the way I felt about it. I feared that speed and showmanship were brutally elbowing aside certain qualities of grace, good taste and composure that we once possessed. I also knew one basic law in nature—that if a species failed to adapt itself to its environment it dies. So for me the question was, how could I adapt myself to what I regarded as degeneration?

Was this not exactly what I was trying to work out in my new novel *Loyal Opposition*? My leading lady was named Serena Gignilliat, another of those unpronounceable Charleston names. She had married John Kennet, a young lawyer from the City of Brotherly Love. But he was not born a Philadelphian and she was shocked to find that he did not belong to the Philadelphia Club nor "go to the Assembly." John had grown up in Harrisburg where his Father had been a Republican state senator and his grandfather a judge of the Superior Court. Very much in love, Serena and John live on Schoolhouse Lane, Germantown where they produced a daughter and a son and give nice dinner-parties. Serena loves to entertain and specializes in Charleston dishes, summer-shrimp pies and sweet-potato puddings. But after five years of marriage they have not broken through the barrier into proper Philadelphia society. As a Gignilliat she considers herself both a patrician and an aristocrat and exclusive Philadelphia was simply going to find that out. True, she had become a member of The Acorn Club and looked forward to capturing a Cosmopolitan Club membership some day. But when John tells her he is leaving his law firm to run for Congress she is furious. As his campaign picks up speed, the telephone rings day and night and John is unable to attend much coveted social invitations. Their marriage begins to come apart.

Not a bad theme, but I wasn't pulling it off. I read the manuscript through from page one to the edge of that terrific chasm no writer can escape—the challenging leap from where you stand firm to all that awaits to be written on the far side of that abyss. There was something else I feared. Plenty of promising novelists hit the jackpot with a first novel, stumble on the second and face the fact that the third is the real test. It's got to be good and *Loyal Opposition* was not.

I told Shippen about the *status quo*. I needed air, I said. He agreed and advised me to set the book aside for a while.

"Oh yes. I know you're supposed to be your own best critic after three months. But three months is forever," I protested.

"Relax. We'll be going up to Maine shortly and you'll have the whole summer to get back into it." He smiled. "Be patient."

I gave him a wry smile in return. Anne Fishburne and I had once discussed our family's besetting sin. "Vehemence," I'd said. "No, impatience" was her answer.

Getting ready for camp was always a happy job. I made lists of food to be mailed ahead to Fernald's store with the date of their delivery, plus a copy to Verna Hodgdon who would put things away. Clothes, shoes, medicines and all our papers (for Shippen was also constantly writing) were packed into suitcases and tucked into the car. There were also all the necessary notes to the laundryman, the milkman and the postman; finally it was the day of departure.

Even happier was the day of arrival. At last we reach the Trenton bridge across the Mt. Desert Narrows with Sargent and Cadillic mountains on the left and "our" Western mountain on the right. A glance down Bartlett's narrows towards "our country" referred to as "the backside of the island" and you fill your lungs with *bona fide* fresh air. The whole concept of life, love and ambition overwhelms you with joy. A thousand memories surge through your mind like a flood bursting through a broken dam: that windy day of a past Pretty Marsh Regatta when the Peppers' boat swamped in the middle of the race and had to be ignominiously towed home; the White-winged Crossbill on top of a spruce tree singing like a wild canary; the endless canoe picnics around Hardwood and Bartlett's islands; Mr. George Wharton Pepper's "Begat Rocks" in Western Bay; lovely, lovely sunlight and ledges and blue water; lovely food, divine swims, and later, everybody on the Sinklers' sunny piazza, or at Gladys and Bill Watkins's point, with the red ball of the sun sinking down behind Bartlett's island. On rainy days, darts, chess, shopping at Northeast Harbor and catching up on Philadelphia gossip brewed by the daily bridge players on School House Ledge, or in those ancient shingle-sided mansions, their glorious gardens lining the eastern shores of the island's picturesque fjord known as Somes Sound. At the head of the sound lies the tiny village of Somesville with its brook flowing under a bridge lined with flower-boxes filled with red geraniums. Here are more houses, our favorite belonging to Bob and Barbara Patterson who live there the year round and have a view of water on one hand

and on the other wide meadows and woodlands. Sitting on their high-up piazza for lunch on a crisp, clear Maine day and settling the problems of mankind in general is just another of the magnetic forces which draw us yearly to Mount Desert.

Summer time! All along the fabulous coast of downeast Maine in thousands of coves, inlets and islets people are sailing, paddling, fishing and crowding their minds with memories of the songs of the winter wren, the hermit thrust and the olive-back. Every outdoor activity provides intimacy with tide and sunset, fog and fen; with coastal meadows brilliant with lupine, wild roses, gold and orange hawkweed, and, at night, with the stars and on happy occasions Northern Lights though I doubt if anyone can claim intimacy with the Aurora Borealis!

A funny thing about all this is that I can't help smiling because at Pretty Marsh I always feel more Philadelphian than I do at home! The reason is absurd. Our harbor is surrounded by Peppers, Madeiras, Grants, Lees, and Strouds on our left, and on our right, by Sinklers, Gibbons, Battles, Ingersolls, Newhalls, Yarnalls, and more Peppers. One might rightly assume that I would be absorbed into all this Phildelphianism. But no! Around the Cogswell point in the Seal Cove area there's a nest of Putnams, Griswolds, Peabodies, Paines and Parkmans, and whenever there are a lot of Bostonians around, I begin to feel audaciously Philadelphian.

To put the finishing touch on this vulgar display of name dropping there are these three declarations:

> Here's to the City of Boston,
>   The home of the bean and the cod,
> Where Cabots speak only to Lowells,
>   and Lowells speak only to God.

and:

> Here's to beautiful Charleston,
>   Where the shrimp look down on the cod,
> And the Hugets speak only to Ravenels
>   And neither speak to God.

and Arthur Guiterman's blythe words:

> When the trees in April quicken
> On the lovely Wissahickon,
> Or in winter where the Schuylkill full of slush
> Cuts the City through the middle
> One may even see a Biddle,
> A Cadwalader, a Shippen or a Rush!

I could not wait for three months to pass before tangling with my problems in *Loyal Opposition*, but fussed with it here and there like a cat with a mouse in its mouth. And when the summer was over and we returned to Navajo Street, I found Philadelphia in an astonishing frame of mind. For years every conscientious Philadelphian had deplored conditions at City Hall, feared Boies Penrose and despised the Vare brothers. A bipartisan movement, sparked by Bob McCracken ("only paupers vote for Roosevelt") urged the need for a new city charter. The more imaginative business men and lawyers of the city finally were able to draw up a Philadelphia Home rule Charter, and in 1951 it was submitted to the voters and approved.

The spotlight then swung over to Chestnut Hill, falling upon Joseph Sill Clark and Richardson Dilworth who had declared their intentions to run for mayor and district attorney. A few months previously Dick had resigned as city treasurer to run for governor and carried Philadelphia but lost to Republican John S. Fine. Although he and Joe had agreed between themselves that Joe would run for mayor first, the party leadership considered that Dilworth was the older of the two and better known. A meeting was held to break this decision to Joe, consisting of city chairman, James Finnegan, John B. Kelly, Frank Myers, James Clark and Albert M. Greenfield. When Joe arrived he refused to be pushed aside and snapped back, "Before we proceed any further I think I ought to tell you that less than an hour ago I released to the press a statement of my irrevocable intention to run for mayor. I intend to run whether or not I have your backing even if my only supporters are my wife and myself. I think our discussion ought to proceed on that basis." The others were taken by surprise but "for the good of the party" gave in.

I had known Joe from way back in our school days. He was several years younger than I, about my brother's age, and I had always regarded him as "too young" to bother about. I was also in awe of his mother, a true grande dame, with a strong will. He went off to Middlesex and Harvard and our paths crossed only in a casual manner until he married Noël Hall, his second wife. Shippen and I invited them to dinner one summer evening and I found Noël lovely to look at, very quiet and very charming. Joe had turned into an attractive man, quick, intelligent and lots of fun, as well as sophisticated.

Dick Dilworth I hardly knew, except that after he had moved into a house on Mermaid Lane just behind my Cresheim Valley studio, he used to jog past my little place and we developed a nodding acquaintance. He was very good-looking and even Joe admitted that. Apparently they had known each other when they were younger on a pleasant basis at

65

Southampton, Long Island, where their families spent the summer. Joe tells us he had always looked up to Dick as a sort of hero. "He was handsome, athletic, and intelligent and when he moved to Chestnut Hill and both of us got into Democratic politics our friendship really started."

Now here they were, both home from the war, teamed up under the title "Independent Voters for Clark and Dilworth" and claiming they could clean up City Hall. The first time I heard them talk I was impressed. The occasion was a gathering at the house of Billy and Louisa Foulke on Rex Avenue, Chestnut Hill, one of many such meetings throughout the city. There was something heartening about their confidence in themselves, something fresh, clean and sincere. After they were through I asked Joe, "What makes you *really* think you can do this?"

"Why not? They've done it in Kansas City, Minneapolis, New Orleans and we can do it here. I'm going to run for mayor and Dick for district attorney. There are lots of Republicans out there who want to see the Vare brothers thrown out and they'll back us. There's also the independent vote. The climate's right for change with so many veterans returning to Philadelphia who realize how backward we are here. Now, with a new home rule charter and your help and people like you it can be done!"

I suppose no historian of those days will be able to avoid a comparison between the two men. Dilworth was warm, volatile, personal and emotional, loving a fight, sincerely caring about people but pulling no punches. Dick was all things to all men—hero, dictator, rough-neck, commando, a knight in shining armor. Joe, on the other hand, wielded a rapier and preferred remote control, but was firm as steel when his mind was made up. Both were sincere about what they had undertaken and made a marvelous team. Dick was the arrow-head of the campaign, removing lids from political garbage cans stinking with sixty-seven years of accumulation and corruption. If some of that splashed up on him, no wonder. Throughout the campaign the voters' reactions were really absurd. One week everybody was saying, "I love Joe and I hate Dick." Next week it would be, "I love Dick and I hate Joe!"

The Philadelphia Record had folded up some months previously, leaving the Philadelphia Democrats without a city-wide newspaper behind them. Dilworth got around this with a neat maneuver of holding street corner rallies. Soap-box orators were nothing new but Joe and Dick made them "news." The first one I attended was with my youngest stepdaughter, Louise Page, on a crisp October evening somewhere down Germantown Avenue near Upsal. We arrived just as the Clark-Dilworth van with its loud-speaker on top pulled up under the harsh glare of an arc light, broadcasting "The Halls of Montezuma" honoring Dilworth's decorations. People began coming out of their houses to see what was going on, and presently both Dick and Joe appeared, climbed on top of the van and, when the music stopped, spread the word in their own magnified voices of who they were and what they intended to do. The setting was theatrical—October wind scattering autumn leaves, the branches of trees swaying near the arc light and throwing animated shadows over the faces of the crowd below. This, I said to myself privately, is what I've got to get into my *Loyal Opposition!* This is what my book needs—something fresh, contagious, sparkling. But was my fictional candidate John Kennet capable of it? Did I have to change him into a Joe or Dick? The whole framework of my book began to shudder. Forget it, forget it for the moment—just watch the real Dick and Joe, how they explain with good humor and determination exactly what they stand for and what against. Just get on with it, get into that over-all heady atmosphere of high adventure which they seem to be able to repeat night after night on the top of their sound truck. Nothing was more stimulating than trailing along with them! And by now, not only the *Inquirer* and the *Evening Bulletin* were giving them much needed publicity, but the street-corner rallies made *Time, Life* and *Fortune.* Mr. Luce personally sent Dick a check for $500.00.

Election Day was victory day for the Democrats and Mayor-elect Clark began choosing the members of his cabinet. I was not alone in being tremendously proud of Shippen's appointment to head up the new three member Civil Service Commission. So were his friends, for he was bound to be a strengthening force in the expanding team of city officials who were to assume office on January 7. With him were Sydney B. Dexter, a Republican and old friend, and the Rev. Luther Cunningham, pastor of St. Paul's Baptist Church, the first Afro-American to serve on the commission.

Editorials all over the country and articles in all current events magazines were applauding Philadelphia's declaration of its own inde-pendence. James Bryce had written in 1893 "there is no denying the fact that the government of cities is one conspicuous failure of the United States." What made Philadelphia's turnabout so significant was the clear fact that we were just about the last big city in the country to heed this criticism.

There was no doubt about it now, we were on our way. Cartoons depicted Joe as the White Knight on a prancing charger, and Dick pulling lids off GOP garbage cans! Our high spirits were revealed in an especially lively manner on New Year's Day, at Albert Greenfield's traditional "New Year's Day Breakfast, from 11 A.M. to 5 P.M." Politically speaking "everybody" was there, wreathed in smiles and bursting with good will towards men, Joe and Dick in particular. I ran into Jim Finnegan, the new president of City Council who made himself most agreeable. What very blue eyes he had! And a pleasant unhurried manner, as if he knew what was expected of him and could deliver. I said wasn't it fun being a Democrat these days, but he replied there would be headaches ahead and I realized some of Joe's appointments, which from my angle looked good, might be bitter blows to the ward leaders and to labor. Shifting from the spoils' system to the merit system would not be easy. Abe Freedman, Joe's future City Solicitor joined us—an alert, keen-minded person with brilliant brown eyes and that special sort of dignified self-confidence characteristic of many small men. I also told him how much I enjoyed being a passionate spectator of this dramatic performance with no responsibility except to enjoy.

"No responsibility?" he exclaimed. "Why, you're our private eye! Our eyes and ears of 1952! You're our historian!"

"Impossible," I replied. "I couldn't be a historian bound by hard facts. I need emotional headway."

Nevertheless Walter Phillips, who had just been made City Representative, took up the refrain and put me to work. They needed someone to keep a record of "who's doing what" in the campaign. Thus a weekly folder called On The Job was born with me as editor. My responsibilities were to visit all local headquarters throughout the city and spotlight people like Marjorie Sturm—the fixed pole-star in main headquarters at 1530 Chestnut Street around which all meteors, comets, constellations and general office chaos swirled. The field work was prodigious— envelopes to be filled, addressed, stamped and mailed. All of this was being done with tremendous enthusiasm inspired by the contagious confidence of "our leaders."

Inauguration Day was to be held on Monday, January 7 at the Academy of Music and in the meantime department heads were frantically setting up their personnel. Shippen began calling Sydney, "the dextrous one," and Luther Cunningham "Martin Luther." And to make things easy on the memory he referred to the department chairmen as "Forde— taxes;" "Baxter—water;" "Recreation—Mann;" "Gibbon—police."

As for me I began cutting things out of the newspapers; making notes, recording conversations. Each department had its own problems, its leaders, being human, bound by their own limitations, family affairs and ambitions. Good heavens! I found I was living in the midst of a hundred novels. Think what could be done with Connie Dallas, first woman in City Council. Think of her opportunities for setting precedents in good taste for the councilwomen who would follow. For example, there was the administration's press cocktail party to be held at the Ritz a few days before the inauguration—traditionally strictly stag. She knew that even one woman would cramp their style. But what to do about her? She solved the problem by not going. Several councilmen banded together and sent her a huge bunch of American Beauty Roses! Then there was the problem of no ladies' room on the fourth floor of the City Hall where she had her office. An immediate solution was promised and in the meantime she was allowed to accept the hospitality of one of the offices across the corridor. Then came the morning when she opened the office door to find, to her dismay, sitting well out from the wall, a glistening white toilet and tank in all its pristine nakedness. One would think that the carpenters would have arrived to put up partitions before the plumbers set to work. It dominated the whole room, and made a farce of grave discussion on political matters. With a constant stream of visitors, all Connie could do was to cover it with her overcoat, scarf and hat.

Connie was to be credited after her term was over with pushing through a new city health code and engineering dozens of major laws. She had a long dispute with Jack Kelly when she permitted fire trucks and police vans to run past his house on Henry Avenue, and she also widened Bells Mill Road at a dangerous curve where flaming youth were wont to smash up their fathers' automobiles. A faithful friend, energetic and generous, whatever Connie undertook she did with style and skill. Her cooking was superb; her entertaining was unsurpassed and her good humor (despite her many problems, especially after George, her husband had several strokes) was boundless. I never heard her complain.

I was reading at this time Robert Sherwood's *Roosevelt and Hopkins* and discovered a parallel to what Joe and Dick were trying to do. Neither of my heroes were FDR or Churchill, but the same tone of confidence seemed to prevail. Our Philadelphia power boys were using their brains and the air continued to be charged with expectations, tensions and ever-increasing drama. History was in the making and how I enjoyed knowing ahead what tomorrow's headlines were going to be! Joe was seeking experienced men from all over the country to head the administration's departments, which instantly enraged many local politicians. Each day some sort of crisis would arise. On the Saturday before Monday's inauguration ceremonies, Shippen spent from 10 A.M. to 4 P.M. at Joe's house on Rex Avenue working over emergency regulations with Buck Sawyer, Managing Director; Len Moak, Finance Director; Abe Freedman; Sydney and Luther Cunningham; and Mike Byrne, deputy mayor. I drove over to Rex Avenue to bring Shippen home and as we got into the car Abe Freedman said to me, "Shippen's enjoying using his brain."

I laughed. "I know he is. And he's told me how wonderful it is to work in politics with fellows like you all who aren't battling for power like ward leaders, but are really concerned about the welfare of the city."

On the way home Shippen explained that the out-going Republican council had voted themselves more pay to take effect on January 2, and that they had to handle this somehow while drawing up emergency regulations. "This affects the firemen, police, trash and garbage collectors—about 12,000 men in all—and maybe they'll strike," he said.

Sunday was just as hectic. Sydney and Shippen were asked to drive to the airport to meet a consulting personnel director from California, Dr. John Fisher. Upon their return to 8018 Navajo Street, they found Alice Male, wife of Shippen's pro-tem personnel director, who had arrived from New Jersey's Department of Institutions until a permanent person could be decided upon. Ray Male was a young man in his early thirties, with a rodent-like face and large thick spectacles which magnified his eyes. Like the rest of us, he was fascinated with the Clark-Dilworth drama unfolding around us.

After introductions were made we all dashed off to Eric McCouch's house for a cocktail get-together affair (Eric's mint juleps were famous), and from there hurried on to the Dexters' house for supper. Finally we were back at 8018 where the Males went to bed in the guest room, Dr. Fisher in the sewing room, and Shippen and I in our bedroom. The telephone rang at midnight. It was Mike Byrne. Another crisis! The oaths of office for Male, Shippen, Luther Cunningham and Sydney had been forgotten! Shippen got me out of bed and I typed them up. Carbons, I thought, would be undignified as each had to be signed by a judge, so I typed up four of them:

OATH OF OFFICE

I _____do solemnly and sincerely affirm that I will support the Constitution of the United States and the Commonwealth of Pennsylvania, and the Philadelphia Home Rule Charter.
Affirmed and subscribed before me January 7, 1952

_____

Pretty amateurish, I thought, but at least somebody caught it in time, and we went back to sleep.

Inauguration Day broke clear and sparkling, and at breakfast, when we told Ray what had occurred at midnight, he slapped his knee and exclaimed "Jacksonian! Positively Jacksonian!" Pretty soon we were picking up Sister Lou next door at 8030 Navajo and were on our way to the Wyndmoor Station of the Reading Line which Shippen had been using because he could walk down from the Reading Terminal to a line of waiting taxis. Once there ourselves, we crowded into a taxi, accompanied by bulging brief cases, the Males' baggage, a huge package of emergency regulations, and the four little typed sheets of official oaths. Arriving at the Academy of Music, Louise, the Males, and I headed for the proscenium box designated for us. Dr. Fisher disappeared with Shippen in the direction of the stage. The Academy was filling rapidly and became jammed to the rafters. The city colors, blue and yellow, were draped below the footlights, and a band in the orchestral pit was making pre-performance noises. I felt I was exactly in the right place at the right time and couldn't wait for the curtain to go up.

It did, on the dot of eleven, and applause broke out like an explosion. There they all were, framed by palms behind and a red carpet out front! Left center, judges and the press; right center, the seventeen members of council and, standing behind them, the commissioners. Center stage, a large and empty armchair awaited the mayor-elect, and Joe's entrance was met with a crescendo of applause. I never saw him look more serious and dignified, as if he'd grown six inches! He was sworn in by Judge Gerald Flood; his inaugural address was sincere and scholarly, and delivered with all of Joe's innate charm. There was no doubt about it, he meant every word he said.

Judge James A. Gordon administered the oaths of office to the seventeen members of council, and the commissioners were sworn in by Judge Curtis Bok. As each official stepped forward to take his oath, place his hand on the Bible and sign his name, the band played the first few bars of "Pomp and Circumstance." It was tremendously impressive and I couldn't help noticing that when Curtis administered the oath of office to Richardson Dilworth, the new District Attorney received the greatest outburst and longest applause of all.

With the ceremonies over and the invocation drawing to a close, Ray and Alice Male and I slipped out from our box and hurried to the Green Room where we found Shippen. Together we went backstage (the curtain was down) and with more "Jacksonian informality" Ray was sworn in by Curtis in a corner among the palms. Waving the fourth little paper I had typed the night before in front of Ray, Curtis said, "You agree to all this?" "Sure!" Ray replied and both signed in the correct places.

71

It was lunchtime now, and I guided the Males across Broad Street to the Ritz where I had arranged lunch for Connie Dallas and George, the Dexters, the Males, Luther Cunningham, Anne and Dick Dilworth, Jim Finnegan, Noël Clark and her mother Mrs. Hall, Frank Myers and Luke Foley, Sister Lou and Andy and Louise Page. Shippen was rushing around elsewhere getting signatures from Joe and Abe Freedman at the Mid-day Club, after the re-writing of those troublesome emergency regulations. For now, the Clark administration was alive, and fully responsible.

After lunch most of us hurried over to City Hall and the Mayor's Reception room to attend the swearing in of the twelve bureau heads—fire, police, licenses and inspection, public property, etc., where judges Robert Bolger and Curtis Bok administered the oaths. After this, Alice Male and I went up to the "new" Civil Service Commission offices. Fortunately Ray Male had a sense of humor, for the situation was fantastic. The room was a flight above the seventh floor where the elevators stopped. City Hall pigeons had clearly been in possession for years. Nests had been found quite literally in the bureaucrat's "pigeon holes!" The place had been cleaned out after a fashion, broken window-panes repaired and a desk and a couple of chairs installed. Frank Brookhauser in his column in *The Inquirer*, "It's Happening Here," reported Ray's first day in office as follows:

> He sat down on a chair. It collapsed. He passed too close to a cactus plant. It cut his cheek. He sat down at his desk, unaware of a corner of broken glass. It cut his arm. Things have to get better, he figures.

But did they? Ray reported to us the next day that a piece of plaster had fallen on him from the ceiling! He sent it to me and I put it on a piece of black velvet and framed it. Ray apparently made a good story out of this to his friend Charles Addams, the famous cartoonist, who drew a horrifying picture which came out in all the newspapers, featuring weirdos coming out of the cracks in the ancient walls of Philadelphia's old City Hall, or crawling up ladders; a stenographer with ashen face and long, long hair sitting at a typewriter; a cat; and a skinny unhappy clerk wearing a visor at work over papers on a desk.

January and February headlines in the papers kept up a steady barrage about all the problems faced by the new administration:

"CLARK VOIDS FORTY HOUR WEEK FOR CITY AIDES."
"COUNTY DETECTIVES FIGHT DILWORTH OUSTER RULING"
*"CITY PROBES CITY SERVICE LISTS, HIRES COMMITTEE OF
SEVENTY EXPERTS"*

72

Ray Male conceded that "many honest and capable people were on the lists in addition to incompetents who had gotten jobs through chicanery." He added that the examinations, for competents, would "give them a chance to show their real worth."

As this sort of analysis, scrutiny and discovery was unfolding in all the departments, the new mayor was displaying a strong ability in what Len Moak, Director of Finance called "a high degree of internal organization." Every department head was told to write a weekly report, which Joe took home every weekend. He then made notes, many of them critical, on things that needed attention. He held his first "Box Lunch Cabinet Meeting" on January 14. Ten earnest and honest men sat around a table in the mayor's inner sanctum and discussed each other's problems. These men were really concerned about the welfare of the city, as Shippen had told Abe Freedman, adding to me later, "Matters of policy are always interesting when they're not selfish ones."

In the middle of March my mother died. On a Sunday morning, Margaret Allen, who had lived with her as a housekeeper, cook and lady's maid, called me up in a frightened voice and said she was ill. Shippen and I went down to 7708 at once and called Dr. Rex. He was out but would be back later. Another doctor came, and Mother asked me why he was there. I could not answer. He diagnosed her illness as a stroke and Mother asked for Shippen to come upstairs. He did, sitting beside her at the bed and holding her hand. By this time I had telephoned Eleanor and she was on her way from West Chester. Dr. Rex came at six o'clock and we engaged a nurse. By that time Mother no longer knew any of us and sank into a coma. Eleanor and I stayed there Sunday night and all of Monday and Monday night. She never regained consciousness, and died peacefully on Tuesday morning. I was deeply impressed with the sublime serenity on her face after she was gone. She looked thirty years younger.

When big moments of life descend upon me, my notebooks fill up with emotional revelations. I felt that Mother had moved on to further adventures with still enough time to look over her shoulder lovingly at Eleanor and me. And before the house was sold and broken up I went down several times to sit in her chair by the window overlooking Father's garden, drawn by the serenity evoked by the memory of her just sitting there, making patience a beautiful virtue.

That spring of 1952 was exceptionally beautiful. How often, only a few years later was I to fill column after column in the then nonexistent *Chestnut Hill Local* newspaper with paeans of praise and joy over spring in the Wissahickon—from the first snow-drops and narcissus to apple-blossoms against the blue of a clean-washed sky! Spring is indeed the symbol of hope, renewing us with energy for all the things we must and hope to do. *Loyal Opposition* was nearly finished, and in April Shippen and I began to get ready for another trip to Switzerland, planning to fly across on June 3, stay in Paris for a few days, thence to Grindelwald and Vitznau. On our return home we'd go directly up to Pretty Marsh: the Democratic National Convention was to be held in Chicago the week of July 20, and we looked forward to listening to it over our radios in camp.

Our plans were never completed. On Sunday morning, May 18, 1952, *The Philadelphia Inquirer* ran the following headline:

"SHIPPEN LEWIS, LAWYER, 64, DIES."

I have read the long clipping often . . . "Death caused by coronary occlusion . . . " All I remember of the funeral at St. Paul's Church, Chestnut Hill, was the tidal wave of voices behind me when the congregation, all standing, recited "The Apostles' Creed." There were hundreds of voices in unison, mostly masculine, the tone and rhythm enriched with reverence, loss and love which will never be forgotten. They told me later after the family had left the church that George Trowbridge, our rector, said there would be silence "until the candles are extinguished."

Bishop Malcolm E. Peabody, our former rector, wrote the following tribute which appeared on the editorial page of *The Evening Bulletin:*

> One could not know Shippen Lewis without feeling that he had
> within him a fount of perpetual joy, nor could one doubt the source of
> that joy. He did not talk of his religion but he demonstrated it in his
> every attitude and every action—in his love of nature, in his kindly
> humour, his concern for others, in his unstinted giving of himself to his
> community and in his loyal support of his church. He was the best of
> friends and the most delightful of companions. To be with him gave
> one new zest for living, and new enjoyment in simple homely things.
> He seemed to carry a plumb line within himself by which the value of
> things, of people, of events, fell into proper perspective. Of his own
> value he thought not at all.
>
> Hundreds came to pay him a last tribute, and he is deemed irreplace-
> able in the posts where he served. Our world needs men of the type of
> Shippen Lewis, dedicated men of integrity, imagination and unselfish-
> ness. May his example help to raise many like him.

Katherine Muñoz sent me Milton's lines:

Nothing is here for tears, nothing to wail
Or knock the breast, no weakness, no contempt,
Despair, or blame; nothing but well and fair.

One very hot summer night in June, Joe Clark came around to see me. We took our chairs from the flagstone terrace around the corner of the house to catch what movement of air we might find. There was dew on the grass, and a distant rumble of thunder in the west. We discussed Kefauver and Adlai Stevenson, and the coming Democratic Convention.

Presently Joe said, "Of course I killed him." After a pause I replied, "No. You did no such thing. Bill Stroud told me he could have been in bed for a year and the same thing could have happened. No. You gave him one of the happiest experiences of his life."

CHAPTER 6
1952–1955

LEAVING CURAÇAO BEHIND us, the Grace Line's Santa Rosa was soon out of sight of land. The deep blue of the Caribbean met the endless horizon with a sharp line against a band of lavender which merged into turrets of opalescent clouds. Eleanor and Butler Windle had invited me to go on a cruise in August, and no ocean liner could be better equipped for such a voyage. At dinner time every evening the glass dome over the dining room split open and each half silently lowered itself out of sight, leaving the passengers at their tables under an open tropical sky glittering with stars.

Romance, adventure, new acquaintances, but not for me. Hour after hour I lay on my shaded deck chair mesmerized by the bastion of cumulus clouds around the horizon which, although nothing but air, trapped me into remembering, and into a grief and loneliness that could not be described.

I had brought with me the field guide to *Birds of the West Indies*, and a book called *Christian Behavior* by the great English writer C. S. Lewis, which helped to keep my wits about me. One thing I'd discovered before I left home—that the poets were more helpful than the philosophers. The latter lived in what seemed like an exclusive Mount Olympus while the poets walked beside you with a comforting arm around your shoulders and a deep feeling of understanding companionship. Certain lines in my own poems amazed me. How could I have written:

I am one with the tossing spray
And the colored rainbows flying!
I am one with the tumbling waves
And part of the sea gulls' crying!

Handfuls of tiny diamonds flung
On the sapphire of the sea
And the trembling colors flashing there
All, all are a part of me!

77

Youth and adventure will never die!
For me there are no fears,
For I am fulfilled in the sea and sky
And go singing down the years!

Would I ever feel again the joy which I put into that *Audubon Magazine* article "Accent on May"? How could I possibly have written at the age of twenty-two a sonnet called "The Gift" when I knew nothing about death and loss? What mysterious forces dwell within us of which we know so little? The thought that Mother was no longer at 7708 Navajo Street and that the house itself was no longer ours was a thought too heavy to bear. All of this blended together with the fact that I would never again find a companionship, a oneness, with another human being such as I had shared with Shippen. Sea and sky? No fears? I was frightened to the depths of my being for there was no one any longer between me and the whole wide world. Even the sea and sky had betrayed me for the surrounding beauty was empty and indifferent to my loneliness.

After only two or three days at sea, struggling to keep up appearances and decent manners, wearing the right clothes at the right time, and trying to ignore the fact I was only half alive, I found the beautiful little ship a prison. I loved my sister and Butler for taking me on this trip, but when I read on the ship's daily newsheet that a two-day bird-watching tour was planned for Venezuela I decided to join it. Shippen and I had loved the bird trips in Florida with Alex Sprunt, and a break on shore was the first wakening of a faint interest in something going on outside the confines of my self-imposed isolation. Perhaps I might add "new" birds to my life list, or possibly find material for another article for the *Audubon Magazine*. The party was to disembark at La Guaira, spend a night in Caracas, drive across country in a van, visit Rancho Grande, a former dictator's palace, rejoin the ship at Maracaibo and proceed to Cartagena, Colombia. Here we would turn around and sail directly back to New York. Eleanor and Butler did not want to come and were a little anxious for me to go off by myself. I said I wouldn't be by myself but with a group which turned out to be seven of us. I took a few notes about the expedition and only recall the abandoned dictator's palace high up in a wild part of Venezuelan forest, a wonderful place for a research station and visited by naturalists from all over the world. I was annoyed with the James Bond field guide because it did not include a fascinating little black and white bird I saw there, which we were told was a "Tyrant of the Marshes." I had no idea that eight years later I would again be in Venezuela and by that time would have learned that the birds of South America and its islands—Trinidad, Tobago, Aruba,

Bonaire and Curaçao—were not related to the birds of the West Indies, so the field guide I'd brought along was useless.

The trip back to New York seemed endless, and the drive along the Jersey Turnpike under the hot August sun, an ordeal. The word Philadelphia meant "home," and in itself aroused in me a sense of belonging at least to something. Eleanor and Butler dropped me off at 8018 Navajo Street, reluctant to leave me, but Margaret McClintock was out front to greet me. Margaret had been with Shippen and me for several years. I had supper on a tray out on the terrace, and Margaret had made my favorite dessert, Junket, which in our childhood we had called "slip-'n-go-down." Everything looked the same. Zinnias were still blooming in the garden and the grass looked its worst after a hot summer. Would this summer never end? Upstairs my desk was piled with mail and on my writing desk was the unfinished *Loyal Opposition*, still to play its part in events to come. The telephone rang and I recognized Sydney Dexter's voice.

"Sydney!" I exclaimed. "How are things going in City Hall? How nice of you to remember when I was coming home."

We arranged for him and Nan to come down for dinner the next night. I called up Marty Adler, another of Joe's ardent admirers, and signed her and Frank up for dinner as well. Marty was very active in the Americans for Democratic Action, but ADA was a bad word at that time along the eastern seaboard, except in Philadelphia where Lawrence M.C. Smith, better known as Sam, and John and Ada Lewis managed to give our Philadelphia chapter an air of distinct respectability.

The next evening I got a pretty clear picture of what was going on in the new administration. Some of the department heads were beginning to rub each other the wrong way, which was inevitable. I asked how Joe was handling all that. There were a couple of signs. Some people still thought Joe a stuffed shirt and arrogant. Those of us who knew him best were well aware of the fact that he was not always diplomatic, that he was poor at coping with irritations and was frequently snappish and abrupt. He wouldn't take the time to make you feel as if it was worth listening to you, so he just impatiently brushed you aside. I doubt if Aunt Kate had taught him to say "thank you" often enough when he was a child. Connie Dallas once said he couldn't laugh at himself. Despite all this he was getting things done. The labor unions had not gone on strike as feared, and he was fair enough to give credit for this to Ray Male, although the glory still went to the administration.

A few evenings later Sam Smith called me up and asked if I would serve as co-chairman with Tom Harvey (a Quaker whom I did not know) on Philadelphia's Volunteers for Stevenson which the ADA was launching. I replied at once that I did not think I could, that I was finishing a book and was very much honored at being asked but . . . . Sam said he understood and we both hung up. I sat there looking at the phone, remembering that Shippen had once said "I wouldn't be surprised if you went into politics one of these days." I also knew that I'd been asked to do things more because of his name than for any notable political ability on my part. Wouldn't getting into the picture have the same effect now and keep Shippen's name and what he stood for in the public eye? I picked up the telephone, dialed Sam's number, and told him I'd be glad to serve.

We opened Stevenson's headquarters a few weeks later at 16th and Chestnut Streets. There were other co-chairmen besides Tom Harvey and me: Dick and Joe, Jim Finnegan, chairman of City Council, and Mrs. Greene. Charlie Hepburn was to raise money, Sam Smith, Leon Shull and Elaine Goff, "ADA-ers," were to run things behind the scenes. Mr. Averell Harriman, who was stumping around the country for Adlai Stevenson, came over from New York with his secretary for our official opening. Tom Harvey, Lew Stevens and I took them to the Pen and Pencil Club for lunch and a press conference. Mr. Harriman's conversation with the reporters, almost a monologue, fascinated me no end and provided me with political lingo and inner sanctum details from which I made notes for *Loyal Opposition*. When asked what plans he might have for after the election, "Honest Ave" replied he had none. Would he like to become secretary of state? He repeated he had no plans. His mind worked slowly but thoroughly and Lew told me later that he was a "walking encyclopedia." Lewis Stevens himself was another distinguished Philadelphia lawyer, active in the Greater Philadelphia Movement and now a member of City Council, a handsome highbrow councilman and a friend and classmate, at Princeton, of Adlai Stevenson.

The next important occasion was the Hundred Dollar Dinner at the Bellevue Stratford. Before dinner there was the usual lengthy cocktail hour where so much lobbying is done. It filled several ante-rooms of The Variety Club, also at the Bellevue. I talked with Judge Gerald Gleason who was warm and overflowing about Shippen. He said Shippen did more "for free" for his country (he didn't say city) than anyone he ever knew, and that his reports on the conscientious objector cases were something they still talked about.

As I wandered into another room with my glass of Dewar's White Label I came upon Joe Clark, Walter Phillips, Councilman Norwitch and one or two others. Joe hailed me, got up, pulled up a chair for me between himself and Walter and exploded a bombshell. "They" had been talking about me that afternoon, he said, and wanted me to run for Congress in 1954.

"Congress!" I exclaimed. "You must be crazy!"

"No. Someone is needed to beat Hugh Scott. We can't take Micks or Schmoes, we've got to take a WASP, so why not another resident from Hugh's very own Chestnut Hill? You can become our Helen Gahagan Douglass, our Margaret Chase Smith. We're serious about this," he went on, "but button up your lips."

"Button up my lips? I should think so! What on earth would I do if I won?"

"Go to Washington. You'd have a lot of fun."

For the rest of the evening I could think of little else. I could no longer lean on Shippen's advice and would have to look at myself inside and out for what I knew myself to be. It wasn't all good. On the other hand I didn't want to close doors through which an interesting or useful life might beckon. Vanity pictured me out front making speeches and writing words of wisdom on current affairs. But what about the things I'd been learning from watching Connie Dallas, her problems as a woman in politics and her door-to-door campaigning which she did so well? I also knew I was very ignorant and that my impatience and tendency to quick decisions would not make for wise judgments. It was "crystal clear" (Joe's favorite expression) that unless I could be as enthusiastic about becoming a congressman as I felt about my writing, I'd do a mighty poor job of representing my constituents. Worst of all, I knew in my bones that I could not possibly go out and solicit votes for myself—for Joe or Dick, for FDR or Adlai, yes, but not for myself.

Frankly I didn't know what I was going to do and continued to be swept along in the high winds of hope that Adlai Stevenson would be elected to the presidency in November. He had defeated Kefauver at the July convention and his visit to Philadelphia was the climax of our efforts in this campaign.

Our group of volunteers for Stevenson and sixty members of the press greeted him on the platform of the Reading Terminal. Among them were Joe and Dick, Elaine Goff, Mr. Brenner, assistant to Earl Selby the columnist, Jim Flanagan and Jack Kelly. I was responsible for taking care of Mrs. Edison Dick, co-chairman of the National Volunteers for Stevenson, and as I was pinning an orchid on Mrs. Dick's lapel, Mr. Stevenson called to her above the heads of the crowd, "Volunteers?" She nodded. What nobody knew was that I had a red rose hidden in my handbag for Mr. Stevenson. As Mrs. Dick had radio engagements she and I did not go with the cavalcade awaiting the others on Market Street at 12th, but took a taxi to her hotel. I told her about the red rose and she said, "Oh, he'd like that!" We agreed that the best time to present it was at the dinner later on. "We'll find the moment and I'll signal to you," she said.

Dinner was at the Broadwood Hotel, a few blocks north of City Hall. When Mrs. Dick and I arrived, there was an enthusiastic mob outside the hotel on Broad Street. Inside she rejoined the Stevenson party. Various people were already seated at the speakers' table on the platform and a large photograph of Adlai was on the wall behind the rostrum and microphones. The hall was packed with a vibrating crowd, the air full of good will and high hopes. I took my place between Lew Stevens and Dick Dilworth at the speakers' table and while waiting for the entrance of the Governor, Dick said something to me again about running for Congress in 1954.

"I'd campaign badly," I said.

"You're a natural."

"Writing's my job. You have to want awfully hard to be a politician."

"True, you do, but you could do both." After a pause he added, "It's a sure thing you'll marry again."

"No it isn't. I like being Mrs. Shippen Lewis, and intend to stay that way."

Then Governor Stevenson arrived, walking down the center aisle towards the platform with Joe, Mrs. Dick, Tom Harvey and others behind them. Mine was the first hand he shook on the stage and I squeezed hard with both my hands. Joe had to wait to introduce him as the clapping and whistling went on and on. Here was our moment! Mrs. Dick glanced at Mr. Stevenson and nodded to me. Although I had to squirm around Dick to do it I managed to hand Adlai an American Beauty Rose bud. He took it, turned to me with a charming smile and put it in his button-hole. Joe gave me a dirty look for getting in the way, but I was pleased to see later on at an overflowing Convention Hall that Adlai was still wearing it.

Those of us who were voting for Adlai Stevenson thought him a great man. His speeches taught us contemporary history. Louise Page said, "You know, after reading his farm speech I understood more about the farmers' problems than I ever believed possible. His facts come before you without ballyhoo, direct from his grasp of the varied issues that concern us." I felt exactly the same way. To be guided by such a man was the chance of a lifetime.

It was not to be. And the defeat was bitterly hard to take, especially when there was a landslide for Stevenson in Philadelphia, his plurality reaching three times that of Truman and even surpassing that given to FDR in 1944. The only bright spot on election night were the comfortable chairs in the Mayor's office as the returns came in. The last thing I heard in bed that night over the radio was Adlai Stevenson's voice conceding the election and quoting Abraham Lincoln's story of the boy who stubbed his toe—"too big to cry but it hurt too much to laugh." I wasn't too big to cry, and wept before falling asleep.

Thanksgiving was soon upon us and I took a holiday from political action by taking my two eldest step-grandchildren, Cary and Esther Page, down to Pinopolis for the long weekend. As the good old Palmetto Limited lumbered southward, floods of memories made me smile as I dressed in my berth, for instead of looking forward to Charleston cousins, beaux, and parties, I was "Granmary" to the two little girls giggling and dressing in the berths across the aisle. Some years later I asked them what they remembered about the visit and all they could recall was the Pullman car, big rooms with high ceilings at Pinopolis and "strange" food!

I finally sent my *Loyal Opposition* to J.B. Lippincott and turned my attention to the social event of the season—the Assembly. Years ago in a book called *Old Deccan Days*, a collection of Hindu stories, I had read a description of the fate of Hindu widows. They were placed in a pit with only a small portion of water lowered to them daily until they died. I decided never to let this sort of thing happen to me. To prove it I would go to the Assembly alone. Knowing how shockingly unconventional this might seem to others, I said nothing about it except to two very close friends, Jean and Francis Chambers (known as "Dutch"). I told them I'd take a room at the Bellevue, slip into the ballroom about midnight through the pantry and mingle with the crowd for a while.

Dutch said, "You'll do no such thing. You'll go down those marble stairs to the patronesses, make your curtsies to them all and do it up in style. Promise?" I loved them for understanding why I wanted to do it this way, and for not inviting me to go with them, and I promised.

It was a restless, curious evening eating supper alone on Navajo Street and reading Somerset Maugham on the train to town. I took a taxi to the Bellevue, registered at the desk, went up to my room, found the rubrim lilies I had sent myself, read, slept, and at eleven-fifteen got up, put on my black satin evening gown (with no back to it), pulled on long pink gloves that went above the elbow, pinned on the lilies, looked at myself in the mirror and mumbled " . . . crazy, going to a ball alone." Stepping off the elevator I walked around the corner and passed the gentlemen's cloak room and then the ladies'. Wearing no evening wrap, I did not go in, but moved slowly among the others, some of whom I knew, toward the spiral honey-colored marble stairway to the foyer below. At the bottom, six patronesses stood in a row, Mrs. Thomas Thacher the first in line, accepting curtsies from the ladies and bows from the gentlemen, every one of them in white tie and tails. When Mrs. Thacher saw me, apparently unescorted, she asked gently, "Are you alone?" I nodded, and as I rose from my curtsy she gave me a tender look of understanding (she knew what it was like to be a widow) and said softly, "We are very glad to see you here." I was warmed almost to tears but managed to get through the rest of the line and turn toward the open ballroom doors.

Charlie Woodward soon had me among the dancers. Stuart Rodman cut in and said that he and Eunice and Katharine and Eddie Clay expected me to have supper with them. I hadn't planned to stay that long but of course I did. Ah—the music! Just listening to it was enough. Only Meyer Davis dared to put *Die Valkyrie* and *Kammenoi-Ostrow* to waltz-time, then shift to *Mighty Lak' a Rose!* I sat in the box with Dottie Nalle, then danced with Eddie Clay, talked with Gladys Watkins from Virginia, had a divine waltz with Mark Willcox, and confabs with Sturgis Ingersoll, Fred Ballard and Sydney Clark. Everybody said the same thing: "I'm so *glad* to see you!"

After supper—scrambled eggs and champagne (it used to be terrapin and champagne) I suddenly left. It's sometimes a good thing to leave a party at its peak—a ballroom floor in rhythmic motion, chandelier aglow, the dancers beautifully dressed for the occasion, the throbbing beat of music turning the whole scene into a harmonious *ensemble*. Smiling a little as I opened my bedroom door I thought, so that's that! Philadelphia's self-conscious gentry at its best! I knew it would be a one-night stand for me and that I'd never do this again.

As for the dignified Assemblies, when the Bellevue Stratford was forced to close its doors some years later, they were programmed (today's computer lingo) to say farewell to the elegant marble stairway, gilded balcony boxes and crystal chandeliers and retreat outside the city limits of old Philadelphia to Bala Cynwyd and the astonishing surroundings of a warehouse belonging to the Adams Mark Motel. *Sic transit gloria.*

Meanwhile, political Philadelphia loyally continued to struggle with the gigantic task of changing over from the spoils system to the merit system. Joe's administration would stand or fall on this problem alone. As Ralph Page put it to me one day, "How's your crowd at City Hall going to keep the racketeers happy? Reform is as unnatural as revolt, and doesn't last. In other words your gambler doesn't want his right to lose his money taken away from him." I always loved to talk to Ralph, especially when he summed up a situation or a person with pithy accuracy, such as his classic description of Clare Booth Luce: "She can act like little Red Riding Hood," he said, "or the Madonna, or Lucretia Borgia. You attack her as Lucretia because she has behaved that way and you try to prove it only to find yourself in the position of attacking the Virgin Mary!"

After a short trip to Charleston and then to join Eleanor and Butler in Florida I came home to find a letter from Starr Cornelius saying with regret that they were rejecting *Loyal Opposition*. George Stevens wrote: "The theme is interesting but the treatment lacks vitality and intensity. I feel pretty much as I would if I went to hear a first rate pianist who had recently decided to take up the violin instead. Satire is your forte and I wish you would write another one."

Satire and vitality! For almost a year now I hadn't had a scrap of satire in me and all my vitality had been spent on trying to keep my head above water. I telephoned Mary Abbott in New York and told her the bad news from Lippincott's and she said, "They are very foolish to lose you." She insisted the book was "not as poor as all that" and that she'd send it to another publisher. Hadn't we heard time and again of a book that had hopped, skipped and jumped from one publisher to another, ending up with a splash in the best seller lists?

Events took a turn in an unexpected direction. It had got about in City Hall that I was writing a political novel and Johannes Hoeber said he'd like to read it. Johannes was a political scientist familiar with Philadelphia politics. Recently he had published two articles in *The New Republic* about Clark and Dilworth. I gave him the manuscript and it took him a couple of weeks to read it. He went so far as to tell me he found it convincing and accurate. Then he threw a hand grenade into the whole scenario by rushing to Bill Rafsky, Joe's secretary, and spreading the word that if *Loyal Opposition* got into the hands of the Republicans it would ruin Joe's career! He was worried about my hero, John Kennet and his love affair with a charming creature in Washington, and the fact that my fictional Serena, John's wife, hated politics and being dragged into public life. It was true that Noël Clark, like thousands of other politician's wives throughout the country, found adaptation to public life hard to bear. But I could not agree with Johannes when he asserted that Billy Bullitt's *It's Not Done* had ruined his political career and that *Loyal Opposition* would do the same thing to Joe. By this time Joe had called me up and said he wanted to read it. I said why not, and he took the manuscript with him on a spring vacation down to Avery Island, Louisiana.

It was spring everywhere, and in the Wissahickon, especially in the Cresheim Valley, neither City Hall's problems nor my book were as important as early morning bird walks, and keeping my position on the second team at Gulph Mills Golf Club. As for *Loyal Opposition*, I was tired of it. It was like trying to save a badly prepared baking dish of spoon bread by adding a little more milk and heating it over again. It also occurred to me that I might be getting out-of-date. I was fifty-four years old and since the second world war a new generation was taking over everything from life style to publishers. My metaphors and quotations tended towards Shakespeare, the Victorian poets and the Bible. I belonged to a certain period and watched some of my contemporary novelists trying, and not succeeding in my opinion, to catch up with modern slang idiom, four letter words in the mouths of "ladies," and explicit sex, and I knew I didn't belong among them. But this did not mean I was ready to give up writing.

Joe came home, returned the manuscript, and scoffed at the idea that it was his story. He added that he'd had a few chuckles and to do with the book whatever I pleased. I talked the situation over with several friends—Sturgis Ingersoll, and a strong Republican, Percy Madeira. Both said forget it. All public men are exposed to gossip, vicious or otherwise. I also discussed it with Ralph Page who understood my point of view and summed it up for me in three words, "taste and intelligence." Knowing in my heart of hearts that George Stevens was right in what he'd said, I called up Mary Abbott, explained the situation to her and told her that I wanted to withdraw the book. She thought I was out of my mind. If I was, I've never regretted it.

A card from Jim Bond postmarked Nassau said he'd be back in Philadelphia early in May and perhaps I'd go birding with him some day. I looked forward to it. I won and lost a couple of golf matches in the inter-club championship; Joe began calling me "Congressman" whenever we met and I began saying, *"Don't* call me that!" And after a long, long talk with Ruben Cohen at the ADA Convention in Washington, who gave me a down-to-earth analysis of what it was like to run for Congress, I reached a conclusion I deeply wanted to reach: that I was not emotionally stable enough to handle Congress without Shippen beside me, and that the big power boys would find a much more capable candidate than me to defeat Hugh Scott.

In mid-summer a little scene unfolded in the Barclay's dining-room. Jim Bond and I came in to have lunch, and at a nearby table Dick

Dilworth was lunching with a friend. When Dick saw us he came over, and as I introduced him to Jim I said, "Dick, I told Joe last night that I'm not going to run for Congress, and this is the reason!" Dick laughed, pressed my hand and said, "Didn't I tell you last fall that it was a sure thing?"

To make things "crystal clear" it was again Katharine Muñoz with the right words. For when I told her it looked as if I were going to marry James Bond, she said, "You'd be a fool if you didn't."

I take a serious view of life at eleven years of age.

As a Nurse's Aide on the roof of the Episcopal Hospital, Philadelphia, during the influenza epidemic, 1918.

Bronze medal from the Philadelphia Browning Society for my poem "The Gift."

The Cresheim Valley's "Walden's Pond," where I worked and wrote for about forty years.

Mrs. George H. Earle, Mrs. Anthony J. Drexel Biddle, and me at the "Only Paupers Vote for Roosevelt" campaign, 1940.

Shippen Lewis—Charcoal drawing by Alice Kent Stoddard

As an Air Raid Warden in Civilian Defense during World War II.

The Clark-Dilworth "Clean Sweep" campaign. Grasping a broom with Dick, Joe, and Jane Freedman.

The Philadelphia Fellowship Commission's "Salute to the Arts" with John Hersey and Spiros Skouras.

Presenting an American red rosebud to Adlai Stevenson at "Volunteers for Stevenson," Philadelphia, 1952.

James Bond skinning European Cuckoo, Barbados, 1959.

The only time Ian Fleming ever met James Bond, Jamaica, 1964.

Autographing *The Petrified Gesture* at Chestnut Hill's
Fireside Book Shop, January 3, 1951.

At my favorite sport, paddling a kayak at our cove in Pretty Marsh,
Maine.

CHAPTER 7

1955–1959

THE CREW HAD rigged up our Yucatan hammock on the stern of the *Lolette*, a coast guard patrol boat put at our disposal by the colonial governor of British Honduras. I was lying in the hammock as the thirty foot cruiser with twin Diesel engines chugged slowly along the shores of Turneffe—a low swampy island off the coast of what is now called Bélize. It was early afternoon and I was mesmerized by the unchanging scenery of mangroves and inlets, my body and mind quietly at peace— an intensive peace. Two terrifying summers were now over, one through loss, the other through the agonies of moving from the past into a future commitment which, as it slowly blossomed, brought me what I was certain could never happen to me again—a true and wonderful companionship.

Now I was on my first expedition to the Caribbean, and found myself in a Joseph Conrad atmosphere, or one of Somerset Maugham's East Indian tales. In fact Jim fitted so well into this atmosphere, perhaps the best way to introduce him is to quote Conrad's description of his fictional character *The Rover* when he wrote: "The course of his life . . . in the opinion of any ordinary person might have been regarded as full of marvelous incidents—only he himself never marvelled at them."

Indeed, when the course of Jim's life is compared to my conventional upbringing, it is truly "full of marvelous incidents." He was born on Pine Street, Philadelphia and baptized at the Church of the Messiah Gwynedd Valley where his parents were spending the summer. When he was five, his father—explorer, rover, and gambler—built a magnificent house in Gwynedd which he named Willowbrook (now the Gwynedd-Mercy College). Its style was colonial—red brick and white pillars set in large grounds with woods, meadows and a stream running through it, all of which required grooms, chauffeurs, valets and house servants.

When Jim was twelve his mother died; Mr. Bond then married an English woman, sold Willowbrook, and, with his two American sons, moved to England to live in an equally grand manner on an estate called Wavenden in Buckinghamshire. Jim went to Harrow and thence to Cambridge, eight formative years of his life which left their mark on him.

After he "came down" from Cambridge, his father, still in touch with his American family, got him a job with the Pennsylvania Company. He returned to Philadelphia and for a time lived with his grandparents, Mr. and Mrs. Carroll S. Tyson at 18th and DeLancey Streets. He was not happy there nor in his work at the Pennsylvania Company knowing that what he really wanted to do was to make a thorough survey of birds in the Caribbean. His father offered to help him but he did not accept the offer. He wanted to be independent and, looking back in later years, realized that if he had accepted his father's offer he would never have learned how to fit himself into the primitive lifestyle of the West Indian native, many of whom became his friends and helped him in ways that no one else could do. He left DeLancey Street and rented a room in a cheap boarding house on Locust Street. Marriage was out of the question, and although he had little money he borrowed enough to join his friend Rodolphe deSchauensee to go off on a six months' expedition to Brazil as field representative of the Academy of Natural Sciences in Philadelphia. On their return they gave some of the snakes, birds and mammals in their collection to the Academy and sold others to various museums and zoos. A Philadelphia newspaper clipping reported an account of the expedition emphasizing "marvelous incidents" with a photograph of Jim entitled "Jungle is His Beat."

He drew up a ten year schedule and stuck to it, spending two or three weeks or more on the larger islands of the Lesser and Greater Antilles, and the Bahamas. If you ply him hard enough you can squeeze out many an entertaining story of his travels on ships, freighters and caiques. He found the German and Dutch ships the cleanest and their food the best, with the worst food of all on the American ships. He spent one Christmas on an American ship among the Virgin Islands. There were only two or three passengers and before dinner the Captain invited them all to the bar for a Christmas drink. In the dining room they sat around one table on which the Captain had placed a tiny Christmas tree.

I once asked Jim why he had specialized in the Caribbean and he replied, "I've always loved islands, the result perhaps of the many summers spent on Mount Desert Island, Maine with my Tyson grand-parents; also, the West Indies, lying between two great continents, are interesting to all naturalists. Nobody as yet had made an intensive bird study there."

Jim's relatives on both sides of the family were not enthusiastic about his profession, except his uncle Carroll's wife, Helen Roebling Tyson who stood up for him. "If he wants to be an ornithologist, why not? That's fine." I first met the Tysons just before we were married when they invited us to a small family luncheon at "Rhodora," their house in Chestnut Hill. The inescapable duty of an engaged couple to meet new relatives can be a shattering performance on both sides but all went well and I was amused at Helen's sense of humor when a lovely set of china was set before us, each plate designed with a pair of love birds.

I knew of course that Carroll Sargent Tyson was one of Philadelphia's distinguished painters and like many other Philadelphians had spent almost every summer of his life in Maine. His landscapes reveal a pleasant intimacy with the meadows, mountains and harbors of Mount Desert Island that he loved so well. He had studied painting in Munich and Paris when a young man and developed an ability to recognize genius among French neo-impressionists, above all Cezanne. Among the many awards during his lifetime he received the Chevalier Cross of the Legion of Honour from the French Government for his "appreciation of French art." He also built a remarkable collection of great paintings and it was always exciting to step into the Tyson house and look again and again at their Van Goghs, Manets and, in the drawing room, Renoir's magnificent *Les Grandes Baigneuses*. The latter is now in the Philadelphia Museum of Art.

I knew very little about Jim when we were married. He told me his father had died in the same year Jim had returned to America. A "marvelous incident" occurred a year or so later when Jim's uncle Neville Tyson left Jim and his brother $25,000 apiece. Brandon Barringer, associated with the investment department of the Pennsylvania Company, and one of Jim's close friends, greatly increased his income and he was able to move away from his drab boarding house to the Crillon Hotel in Rittenhouse Square, much to the relief of his family. He continued his regular expeditions to the Caribbean, and in 1936 the Academy of Natural Sciences of Philadelphia published his first book, *Birds of the West Indies*. A few years later Thomas Barbour, internationally known zoologist at the Museum of Comparative Zoology at Harvard, wrote, in his *Cuban Ornithology*:

> A noteworthy event in Antillean ornithology was the decision of
> James Bond of the Academy of Natural Sciences of Philadelphia to the
> study of birds of the West Indies. A peerless observer and a person of

97

great charm of manner he made himself welcome wide and far. Feeling that less collecting and more observation of birds was the need of Antillean ornithology, he devoted himself in a leisurely way to studying the abundance, breeding habits and distribution of the birds of the Antilles, so that he may now rest sure in the knowledge that no one has ever lived who has seen as many Antillean birds as he has or seen them as intimately.

I pounced on the word "leisurely," for travel to me meant carefully laid plans and reservations made well ahead of time. Jim accepted this approach while travelling in Europe which always included England where we would see his two stepbrothers and stepsister. On the continent, Switzerland was one of our favorites, especially the Engadines where the air is magic like the air of Shangri La. You can walk there forever in lush green meadows knee-high with wild flowers and never get tired. The mountain lakes are very cold but those of us who think nothing of diving into frigid Maine waters take it in our stride.

But travel with James Bond in the West Indies is a different story. The islands are his stamping grounds and he is at home in all of them. Each visit has a definite objective but the approach is leisurely, often with no hotel reservations in advance. Plans are easily changed at the last minute, and time limits on each island become a matter to be decided after we get there. I found this sort of thing a little disconcerting at times. "There's always a place to stay" he would say soothingly, but I would reply, "It's always comforting, don't you think, to know at least by lunchtime where we are going to lay our heads at night?" I'm glad to report I never had to sleep on a park bench, hang my hammock under a sheltering palm, or on the deck of a ship. Indeed I became very fond of the little old-fashioned hotels Jim loved and every year I burst into enthusiasm over each new-to-me island revealed in letters to my sister Eleanor. Of St. Lucia, I wrote:

Sitting at our window in the St. Antoine Hotel is like sitting in a balcony box at the opera. Dawn is always exciting: cathedral bells jangle, a thousand cocks are crowing, the curtain goes up and the sun's exploring fingers press between dark green foothills and reach the tinted warehouses along the waterfront, then pick up the sails of the fishing fleet tripping over the dark green harbor like a flock of small white moths. Already endless streams of natives flow along the roads into town, women toting baskets on their heads heaped with fruit and vegetables. At nightfall, after the caiques have drifted home laden with flying-fish, the dark streams of humanity will be reversed, toiling up the roads into foot paths to their huts, their 'ground provision' having been exchanged for the fruits of the sea.

Or, from Martinique:

It's like Algiers here but not as much money and reminiscent of
Charleston with beautiful iron gates and fine old 'great-houses' in the
residential section. We spent our first night in Le Vieux Moulin, once
a sugar mill, then the governor's house, now a hotel. And the view! Just
after sunset the light had a miraculous quality, low and golden. Palm
fronds glittered like sabers. Below us the harbor was deep in shadow,
the water a rich dark green. A freighter moved out slowly with dignity,
destination unknown. Behind us in the purple-shadowed hills the silver
domes of a cathedral were set on fire by a fugitive shaft of sunlight
escaping through a dip in the dark sky-line.

New worlds to explore! To enjoy! To write about! Islands, islands
born of the sea! Martinique, standing on a submarine ridge with great
deeps plunging down on both sides evoking a thrilling sensation of ocean
floors sinking and rising, of shore lines receding and advancing, and of
vast gases building up inside, threatening to burst into volcanoes! And
Dominica! When seen from the air, Dominica overwhelms one with a
romantic challenge to explore its deep ravines, as if an Olympian hand
had crushed a piece of dark green velvet and dropped it on the surface
of the sea! Each glimpse into those dark hollows, smothered in exuberant
vegetation, sends a kind of shiver up the spine!

And the hospitality of the islanders! As our yearly visits wove themselves
into our lives, there were five hotels that made us feel at home—very
much as home. The beautiful Mona Great House stood on a rise of
land like a white queen, its patio and terraced gardens facing Jamaica's
famous Blue Mountain range. At the sprawling old-fashioned Marine
Hotel in Barbados, you could sit on the wide porches at tea-time and
listen not only to the soft plop of tennis balls on the grass court, but also
to the incessant cooing of Zenaida doves. How we loved both the St.
Antoine overlooking the harbor of Castries, St. Lucia, and the very old
Santa Maria in Grenada, soon to be called the Islander, and all too soon
to crumble away and be closed, even to old-timers. And the fifth, the
Queen's Park Hotel in Trinidad, with its two elderly lady clerks at the
desk who made you feel like members of the Queens' Park family, and
gave you a card to The Trinidad Country Club.

There was a special rapture in discovering one's own West Indies.
The overwhelming intimacies of the natural world in all its wonder: sun,
tides, wind, and ever-changing shorelines; moon and stars at night; all
continuously obeying laws which lift the spirit into a marvelous sense of
cosmic equilibrium. Indeed, I found myself back on an old familiar trail

of beauty, rhythm and harmony, and how fortunate I was to share with Jim the tail end of that pre-tourist period which he knew so well.

But after one's first fine rapture of discovery, a few unpleasant aspects become evident. I would never want to keep house in the West Indies. All hot countries have similar problems, and everyone grows weary of certain ants in the sugar. The dragging tempo of life year after year in the deadly monotony of unchanging seasons, the heat, and the lack of education makes for an inarticulate, groaning kind of humanity, sharp and ugly here and there with apathy and disease. How appalling the wasted hours, the "near enough" philosophy. How tiresome the shabby paint, cracked linoleum floors, garbage dumps behind hotel kitchens, and live rats picking up scraps from open drains, and, most tiresome of all, the incompetent plumbing.

But changes in the West Indies were soon coming. The travel industry experts were prophesying a Golden Age for the Caribbean, very different from the kind of gold the islands used to offer. Even the traveller was changing. As V.S. Pritchett recently remarked, "The old time traveller was generally welcome because he was a rare being. Today no one's a traveller any more. We are all tourists and tourists aren't rare. They swarm." For a while it was gloriously true that "getting there is half the fun." The mood was constant carnival. The Caribbean sky was becoming streaked with the white feathery wakes of planes carrying enthusiastic sun-worshippers into every island in the sun, each island development group prophesying that "our" island is bound to become *the* mecca of West Indian tourism. Magazines, newspapers, stories and novels about the West Indies flooded the newsstands. Nature guides to tropical flowers, birds, seashells, butterflies, fishes and the geology of the region began to jump to astronomical numbers. Come to Barbados! Come to Bermuda! Fly to Grenada! St. Kitts! St. Lucia! Fly BOAC! Fly Yellowbird with Eastern! Fly KLM, and the Pan American Clipper Ship!

We, too, were caught up in the carnival spirit and spent many enchanting hours island hopping and running into people we knew, not with the attitude of "fancy seeing you here," but with the general acceptance of the unexpected, the bizarre, the exciting. But each time we returned we could see and feel the changes, so many to our sorrow. When the St. Antoine Hotel burned down, we almost cried. When the Mona closed its doors because its surroundings were being turned into a development of "town houses" and condominiums, we were deeply distressed, and when the Marine Hotel in Barbados was taken for government offices, we just shook our heads in despair.

The fact that our favorite haunts were slipping away into oblivion did not mean we were no longer making our yearly trips to the West Indies. For Jim there was always something new to record. As Oliver Austin pointed out in the preface to his *Birds of Japan*, the production of a faunal work is often out of date before it is off the press. I was pleased with this aspect of Jim's profession. A politician's career can end overnight in a lost election, and a judge can come to the end of his term, but, like the artist, a naturalist's work is never done.

The West Indies islands were not the only place where things were changing. Philadelphia was heading into an exciting period of reform and renovation. Democrats and Republicans worked together to draw up a new city charter. Dick Dilworth began challenging the Republican City committee by exposing scandals in high places, and Ed Bacon, executive director of the Philadelphia Planning Commission, was drawing up plans for vast changes in physical Philadelphia. The next thing we knew the Chinese Wall had been torn down and the Penn Center Complex of high-rise office buildings and apartment houses had gobbled up Pennsylvania Railroad's Broad Street Station. Now we hopped off the Chestnut Hill local in the underground Suburban Station, took an escalator to street level and looked around trying to figure out where we were.

As for changes in Chestnut Hill, all kinds of things were going on, especially for Jim and me. We moved out from town into an amazing house on Davidson Road. I have lived in four different neighborhoods in the St. Martin's area and had decided long ago that if I ever had anything to do with building a house it would have to be on the edge of the Wissahickon. Consequently when we decided to move back into the scenes of my childhood, we thought George Woodward, Jr. might have some ideas, and he had. The Henry estate, "Stonehurst," between Dr. Woodward's "Krisheim" and Mr Houston's "Druim Moir," was being turned into a development now known as "Cherokee." Oscar Stonorov was the architect of the new two-story apartments and I asked George if we could rent two apartments one above the other and put a circular stairway between them. Oscar, I pointed out, would be only too delighted to create a dramatic stairway.

George regarded me over his eternally crooked spectacles and said, "What about a house?"

"A house? Where?"

It turned out that they were putting a new road through the development to be named Davidson Road after Donald Davidson Dodge, husband of Gertrude Henry. Fortune smiled on the project. Papers and leases between Woodward Inc., D.D. Dodge, Oscar, and ourselves were drawn

101

up and signed and I was beside myself with joy. And how lucky to be married to a man who wasn't too particular where he lived and took little interest in architecture! I could have everything my own way! But I must say I could not make head or tail out of the blue prints Oscar showed us, and as the house began to take form and substance I was secretly alarmed. I took comfort in the fact that we were not paying for it but only renting on a ten year lease with the option of buying the house at the end if we so wished. This was one of the Woodward unique arrangements which included a clause to the effect that a certain percentage of the ten years' rent would be deducted from the final purchasing price.

Oscar insisted upon calling his creation a "cottage." It was built of soft rosy brick, glass and aluminum tucked into the side of a ravine. The flat roof was but one foot higher than the street. The next level was down about eighteen steps to car-port, kitchen, spacious front hall, dining room, porch, and a small bedroom and bath. On the ground level were two bedrooms, a large bath and a huge living room twenty feet high. One end wall was solid brick inside and out; the other was composed of glass and on two sides aluminum. I faced the problem of twenty foot high curtains! Outside were patios, and terraces sloping down toward the site of the Henry swimming pool, now empty, cracked and full of fallen trees. A woodland area of tulip poplars towered over the whole area.

The stairways were appalling—one outside from porch to patio, the other inside from front hall to living room. A huge mahogany beam ran the length of the house through the wall to the patio from which Oscar hung slender black iron rods like harp strings attached to slabs of pine wood that served as steps. It took courage to walk up and down these contraptions but we got used to them. A cottage? A monstrosity in my eyes! But it was on the edge of the Wissahickon!

We planted pine trees, flowering shrubs, Japanese maples, dogwoods, rhododendron, laurel, barberry bushes and holly. It took a few years for them to take hold but each spring it was a joy to see them flourish. In fact, for a dozen years or so it was quite a lovely place, its theatrical personality crying for large entertaining. Occasionally we lived up to its expectations, but preferred to see our friends in smaller numbers.

Julia Henry, Chestnut Hill's most glamorous grande dame at this time, came to call one day. She brought a bottle of vintage sherry as a house warming present for Jim, and for me a charming little pitcher covered with violets. Her eyes grew wide as we showed her the place. Standing at the mahogany beam railing of the dining room, she looked

102

out through the spacious windows over the property which she knew so well as Mrs. Charlton Henry, and in a lilting voice exclaimed, "Is *this* Chestnut Hill?"

Moving back into my former habitat I fell easily into the familiar routine. How pleasant to renew friendly contacts with various butchers in the grocery stores as well as with milkman, postman, laundry man and "The Fabulous Shops of Chestnut Hill." I'd been keeping up after a fashion with what was happening in City Hall and was pleased when Dick Dilworth asked me to introduce him and Joe at a large luncheon of the Philadelphia Citizens' committee at the Barclay. And when eight hundred mayors and two hundred and fifty wives came to Philadelphia to attend an American Municipal Association conference I was again delighted when Joe asked me to be chairman of the hostess committee. It was quite an occasion starting out at the Bellevue with a big dinner, and ending up in the Art Museum where we attended a "Town Meeting of the Air," and *danced* on the museums grand Stairway!

Joe's term as mayor was coming to an end and it was expected the turnover to Dick would be a smooth one, and it was. Joe had made it "crystal clear" that he would serve only one term as mayor. After Dick easily defeated the Republican candidate Thatcher Longstreth and was inaugurated in January 1956, Joe put all his energy and expertise into capturing the seat he coveted in the U.S. Senate. Before he left the mayor's office he appointed me a life member on the Board of Trustees of the Free Library of Philadelphia to fill the place Charlie Woodward had just left. I was deeply touched by what has proved to be a long association with the library, convincing me that free libraries are almost more important than universities.

During all the changes that were occurring in my life I was still using the Cresheim Valley studio as the focal point of my writing, and was extremely busy writing up our West Indian experiences. With a book in mind, mostly for family and friends, I rounded up various articles that had appeared in the *Audubon Magazine* and *Frontiers*, which eventually were printed and called *Far Afield in the Caribbean*. When, I wondered, would I be able to settle down long enough to tackle another novel? New friends, new relatives, new house, new pleasures, new habits! We were spending more and more time each summer in Maine, going up in June and returning after Labor Day to "put our house in order," domestically speaking, then taking off again for Pretty Marsh to be in time for the opening day of grouse shooting, October 1.

This was a must for Jim. For years he had spent every fall game-shooting with his uncle Carroll and a group of hunting friends. They stayed at Carrolls' unique Shottie's Camp near Southeast Harbor, and at his hunting camp in Greenfield—a small cabin in an apple orchard. One of the trees was a "snow-apple" that produced the most succulent applesauce ever known to man.

About half a mile away one entered the real "Maine Woods," a wilderness through which ran a thirty mile CCC (Civilian Conservation Corps) road used almost entirely by lumbermen and hunters. Every so often an old logging road, overgrown and scarcely recognizable as a thoroughfare, ran off from the CCC road into the wilderness. One such road was known by Jim's hunting group as The Dollar and a Half Road because it was mile and a half long, and never failed to produce good shooting. Now that Jim and I were married, it became our habit to return directly to Pretty Marsh every October, where he would leave me at our camp for four or five days, and join the stag hunting party (stag in this sense meaning no ladies). After returning with his share of the bag of grouse and woodcock, we would do some hunting together on Mount Desert Island.

Three years after our marriage his uncle Carroll died and Jim took me back into the Greenfield territory. What wonderful hunting days they were! Snappy October air! Terrific pull of adventure and the unknown just around another bend in the track! Eyes alert on both sides for the slightest movement of those wily birds so hard to outwit that you salute them with respect because they are smarter than you are. Shade and sunlight; old marks of jeep tires in a muddy place; soggy sections to cross, or walk around, or jump over; the harsh cry of a Canada jay; the chatter of a squirrel . . . I always walked behind Jim and perhaps no man has ever had so many pictures taken of his back. One of my favorites is his figure in a birch grove, knee-high in goldenrod and thistles, every line of his back and shoulders, raised elbows, and forward thrust of his head, on the alert, tense with expectancy as he steps cautiously forward. Around him the slender trunks of white birch trees, their delicate foliage now yellow, quivering against the cold blue sky.

Then back to the car on the CCC road, a picnic lunch on a sunny ledge, a bit of hunting on the way back to civilization and finally the long drive home at dusk past blueberry fields now purple-red, and a huge golden harvest moon rising slowly over the ragged lines of spruce and hemlock along the roadside.

As for eating grouse, that must be done with great ceremony. It is always an occasion. At our camp it goes like this: the bird, having hung for four or five days, has been plucked by Jim and is now in the oven.

A few minutes before it is ready Jim is outside on the big porch struggling with the wire and cork of a bottle of Mumm's champagne. The sun is setting over Bartlett's Island and the clouds overhead are beginning to turn lavender and pink from the afterglow. I come out with a small plate of grouse livers on two tiny pieces of home made melba toast. On four other pieces of toast are a dab of Philadelphia cream cheese topped with real Romanov black caviar. I hurry back to the refrigerator for two chilled champagne glasses, rush outside just in time to hear the pop of the cork which flies out over the barberry bushes into the sea. We drink two not quite full glasses of champagne, toasting the bird, the people we love, Pretty Marsh and ourselves, finish the hors d'oeuvres and go inside. The bird is put on the table accompanied by cranberry jelly, a tossed salad of lettuce, radishes and watercress. Fat, succulent, cooked forty-five minutes with a filling of onion, cracker crumbs, Scotch Bonnet, black pepper and melted butter—*this* bird provides another occasion to be long remembered. At that moment Eisenhower may be setting up campaign headquarters in Gettysburg; Adlai Stevenson's hat may again be in the ring, Dilworth is mayor-elect, and Clark will now challenge Duff. But to-night, ruffed grouse is the news! Oh boy! And how many of the above named know a single thing about that wild-flavored meat!

Hunting was a new experience for me. I had frequently listened to my southern cousins chattering in their animated way about fox hunting, deer hunting, and adventures with quail, duck and turkey. I had heard endless boasts about hunting dogs and the sly swapping off of a poor retriever on a friend or cousin one did not like. I also heard them praise their own hounds with passionate affection except, when at 2 A.M., kennels vibrated with the clamor and ululation of bored and lonely retrievers. At Pinopolis when this happens, my dear cousin Doc Fishburne steps out from his front door in his pyjamas and, with an impressive roar, southern accent and all, commands them to shut up and they do.

I was also impressed with plantation gun-rooms, usually a small room off the main hall, very cozy, with comfortable leather-bound chairs and couch groups around a fireplace. On the walls are hung hunting pictures and racks for guns and rifles. Open a table drawer and inside you'll find boxes of cartridges and a hunting record that may go back a generation or more. Over the fireplace there may be a deer's head or a pair of fine antlers. Small bronze figures of fox, hare, hound, or horse may adorn the mantelpiece, along with a pair of stuffed quail under a glass dome. On a table in some dark corner a gorgeously painted decoy duck may catch the eye. At Medway, the Stoney plantation, I once saw blood-soaked shirt-tails hanging on a hook, proof of someone's having just killed his "first deer." I am glad to say this trophy was on display only temporarily.

Jim was thoroughly at home among the hunters, game and guns, and he enjoyed our visits to South Carolina. He still talks about a large platter of teal, canvas-back and redheads, after a bowl of she-crab soup, presented to us by our cousins Emily and Ben Scott Whaley in their house on Church Street. Jim also likes to recall his shooting days while he was at Cambridge University. As the only American member of the Pitt Club he often speaks of the wonderful days of shooting in the hills and hedgerows of the English countryside. He even kept a dog at the time, a black Labrador retriever–the "dog-love of his life"—named Stripe, because of a long white stripe down her chest.

Jim's most prolific shooting experience was in Cuba when his friend Gastón Villalba took him duck hunting on the southern coast of the island. They would leave Havana before dawn in a car, drive to San Cristobal, and from there take a narrow-gauge railway car through the cane-fields to a friend's hacienda where horses awaited them. They rode all day long and finally reached the south coast and another farm where they spent the night. But they were up again before the sun and were off, after a cup of coffee, to the lagoon. There were no decoys and the ducks were so plentiful and flew by so fast in such masses the sport was called "pass-shooting." The limit allowed was one hundred ducks per person per day! King George VI would have been in his element; some of his famous shooting parties recorded over 1,000 ducks for the day's "pick-up." Jim says he never shot more than a dozen.

A very different story is pheasant shooting, Philadelphia style. Although game shooting within the city is forbidden, Philadelphians who loved the sport were able to enjoy it on private properties outside the city limits. On "our" side of the Schuylkill river—the Whitemarsh Valley, Pennlyn, Bethayres, Huntington Valley side—a small group of shooting enthusiasts used to meet on Saturday afternoons during the fall and winter at one another's country estates and make a social occasion of their sport. For Jim and me, just back from the glorious autumn woods of Maine, the plunge into the speeded-up tempo of life in our big city was made easier by these frequent afternoons spent in the lovely rolling hills of our neighboring countryside. What a delight it was to drive up to Joe Lippincott's house, "Oak Hill" in Bethayres, to find others who had arrived before us, sit down to one of Virginia's unforgettable luncheons and listen to conversation reminiscent of Carolina talk of guns, setters and retrievers. I loved seeing the men in hunting clothes—turtle neck sweaters under hunting jackets, whipcord trousers, boots, and, later, out-of-doors, tweed hats and red hunting caps. There was something Trollopian about it when, after lunch, the hunters and their dogs (the latter very impatient) stood at the edge of a cornfield waiting for Joe to designate each man's post.

We were often at Welsh Meadows where our friends Jean and Dutch Chambers lived. Jean was always on hand to greet the guests on those Saturdays when the shoot was to be held on their place. Again one could not help thinking of Trollope and the hunting scenes in his many novels. A large wide-spreading sycamore stood between the old stone house and the barn and kennels, setting the stage of act one for the afternoon's event. Cars drove in and parked in the sunflecked shade; out would step Cliff Cheston with his black Labrador, or Mr. George Widener with his beautiful golden retriever. One after another they assembled, Owen and Alix Toland—Alix a tiny figure in her shooting clothes among the men; or Charley Biddle; Henry Coxe; Joe and Bert Lippincott; perhaps the Pitcairn brothers; or the current British consul if he were a game hunter. All were good shots, and a few were great shots. Charley Biddle was possibly at this time "the greatest shot around Philadelphia." In fact, his reputation was such, that when Jim and I were in London one time, the son of Billy Collins, our publisher, rushed up to Jim and said, "Philadelphia? Do you know Mr. Charles Biddle?" Jim nodded and young Collins exclaimed, "He's my hero! Has been since I was a lad. We met him in Scotland, and he's the best shot in the world!"

What I enjoyed on those long ago occasions was being in open countryside with congenial people. I loved the sunlight on the yellow cornfields surrounded by grassy slopes on the edge of autumn woods, not as bright as the Maine woods but pretty good for Pennsylvania! I loved the summer night dinner parties on Jean's terrace, and many other occasions when we were there. I loved Welsh meadows, and as the afternoon went on and the shadows lengthened across the fields and meadows, the barn and house from a distant rise of ground took on the quality of a landscape Andrew Wyeth might have painted.

CHAPTER 8

1959–1963

AS MY WEST INDIAN notebooks began to pile up I couldn't help thinking I was ready to tackle a novel in that setting. I had packed them with descriptions of people we had met; with incidents amusing, tiresome and delightful; with flowers, fruits and plants; and reports in local newspapers of strange habits and actions of the islanders—all of which, if handled skillfully, could make a colorful and dramatic background. Almost every day you could find in the local news reports of jealous women who had thrown acid in the face of a rival; of snakes and poisonous spiders slipped into the bed of an enemy; or of setting fire to someone's cane fields. Jim's remark that there were only two kinds of women recognized by the islanders—the lady and the prostitute—gave me the idea that a normal modern American girl of the 1950's, naive, independent, and confident that the American lifestyle was superior to all others, might easily get herself into a bad mess, possibly to the point of causing trouble internationally.

On the other hand, Alec Waugh, in his *Island in the Sun*, had masterfully covered just about every melodramatic situation among the people of the Caribbean, socially, politically, racially and morally, while I subconsciously was on the shaky side of trying still again to master the intricacies of fiction. I had given up on the short story, having discovered that articles in the first person singular brought me more success. It was pleasant indeed to find some of these articles about our excursions into the Caribbean appearing in the Sunday edition of the *New York Times* "Travel Section," the *Audubon Magazine* and other publications. I was also facing up to my limitations, accepting the fact that the Great American Novel was not going to spring from my brain.

I was deeply interested in Jim's work and was becoming familiar with the titles of some of his papers, such as *The Derivation of the Antillean Avifauna* and *The Zoögeography of the Antillean Region*. I had never

109

heard of zoögeography and looked it up in Webster's dictionary, which said: " . . . a study of the distribution of animals over the surface of the earth," a perfect description of what Jim, through birds, was doing in the Caribbean. This led eventually to his identifying the exact geographical line between Grenada and Tobago that separates North from South America. It now has universal acceptance among naturalists and is called "The Bond Line."

One evening when we were at home, I was reading the *Evening Bulletin* and, on an inner page, Jim's name caught my eye. I read on, then turned to him and asked, "What's the Brewster Award?"

He replied, "The highest honor an American ornithologist can get."

"Well, you've got it!"

"Don't be frivolous," he replied, thinking I was joking. I handed him the paper and he read it, tossed it aside on a chair and began to walk the floor. "This will help my work," he said.

It did not seem to bother him that this was an odd way for the American Ornithologists' Union (AOU) to inform a recipient of its most coveted medal. I remembered that a year before we were married he had received a British citation for his work in the West Indies, the Musgrave Medal, which had been presented to him with great ceremony in Jamaica. But I was thrilled, realizing how much this would strengthen his authority and prestige, and, although the Academy of Sciences never even said "Boo-Dadday-Boo" about it, his friends began calling him up and congratulating him. Weeks later he was informed of the honor and asked if he would like a bronze medal with a generous honorarium or a gold medal with a small monetary prize. He chose the latter.

Not long after this he was awarded the Wilderness Club medal, given by a Philadelphia club that brought together sportsmen, big game hunters, nature photographers, natural scientists and travelers to remote regions of the world. They frequently held their annual dinners at the zoo; and on the occasion when Jim was about to be handed the medal from the club president, Philip Ward, one of the lions behind the tables let out a mighty roar and everybody laughed. The menus at those dinners in the early years often featured bear meat, walrus steaks or buffalo filets. Now-a-days they have retreated to capon and Virginia ham after snapper soup.

Jim took a great interest in my writing but I was wildly jealous of him because everything he wrote got into print—not only in the Academy's *Notulae Naturae* and *Proceedings* but in *The Auk*, the AOU's magazine; the *Ibis*, the British Ornithologists' Union magazine; *The Wilson Bulletin* and elsewhere.

But for me, something lay in wait which I could not have imagined, starting with a letter I received one summer while at Pretty Marsh from Jean Ballard Wells. She wrote that several ambitious young people (like herself) were trying to start a newspaper to be called *The Chestnut Hill Local*. When I returned from Maine in the fall would I become a member of the editorial staff and help them out? Remembering my *On Leave* news sheet for servicemen during World War II, I wrote back to Jean that anyone courageous enough to start a newspaper in Chestnut Hill deserved all the encouragement they could get. So I joined them in September.

"What a guileless, rollicking, crusading time we had!" Editor Ellen Newbold wrote. "It was young Harry Valentine, Jean Wells and Pat Lowery who brought the paper through the first fifteen months. But Harry moved on to a teaching career and Pat to become secretary of the Community Association, which left a triumvirate of three to carry on— Jean, Mary Wickham Bond, and I."

Of course it wasn't just we three who were running things. Homegrown talent, as Jean put it, was deeply involved—Chestnut Hill's artists, cartoonists, novelists, writers and poets, doctors, lawyers, bankers, historians and housewives. And the newspaper, we knew, was only a part of the overall project to "keep the village tidy" and secure improvements for everyone.

The coordinator of this massive undertaking was a mastermind known as "That Man from St. Louis." His name was Lloyd Parker Wells, a World War II aviator who had "discovered Chestnut Hill" some years before and was determined to save it from "neighborhood blight." In so doing he earned for himself the names of "Gadfly, burr under the saddle, visionary, idealist and a damn nuisance."* He distributed what he called a zip code report on the different groups dedicated to the preservation of the "Wonderful World of Chestnut Hill," entitled "Six Pillars of Chestnut Hill: The Community Centre, the Community Association, the Development Group, Water Tower Recreation Center, the Chestnut Hill and Mount Airy Business Association, and the Parking Company." As coordinator of all these groups he confronted plenty of problems, disagreements, jealousies, prejudices and friction. But he got things done and hypnotized many others to help him. He was wizard, necromancer, sorcerer—a veritable Svengali sitting upstairs in his *sanctum sanctorum* on the second floor of the community center pulling strings and knocking

---

* *Chestnut Hill Local* editorial, May 1978

heads together and making a considerable number of localites dance like marionettes, some with spritely glee, others crazed with rage.

Once inside that holy place, he would offer you a chair, sit back in his own behind his desk and wave his arms toward huge maps on the walls exposing his plans for Chestnut Hill. Overflowing with charisma, he was also experienced in the hypnotic art of convincing you that *you* and *you only* in all of Chestnut Hill could perform a certain service essential to *his* particular dreams!

Although engrossed with the West Indian novel I had finally tackled, he set me to writing a series of Garden of Eden fables, carefully forged weapons aimed at cleaning out pockets of prejudice which were holding up his plans. We worked up a mixed bag of *dramatis personae*, naming the imaginary characters after streets in the community. The project was introduced by the following paragraph:

> The editors wish to call the reader's attention to this, our first of a series of 'Fables' concerning a present day suburban community, and its genuine and imaginary problems that beset it. Subsequent 'Fables' will appear in future issues of *The Local*.

The serpents in this Eden were prejudice, misunderstanding, ignorance, snobbery and self-interest. But such was the overall spirit of the community that we believed we could arouse enough of those who truly cared about the future of Chestnut Hill to unite into outwitting the serpents.

There were seven of the fables, and at the end of each, was the question in white letters inside a black box—What price prejudice? For example, there was Mr. Roanoke who thought that Mr. Willoughby Grove, head of the Development Group, high-hatted him, and, to "get even," he built his ultra-modern bank of glass and chromium in the middle of Eden's Colonial Row of shops and restaurants, thus ruining the "country town store" atmosphere. There was Mr. Lane Hartwell who, because of a private grudge against Mr. Meade Moreland, refused to sign his name on any paper that included Mr. Moreland's name, thus holding up a much needed parking lot behind their adjoining backyards. As for Mrs. Rex Crittenden, one of those wealthy, exclusive lingerers from the Victorian era—she, poor dear, lost her cook because she put up a high fence so the Hampton kids couldn't "spoil her view" when they ran across her lower lawn with friends just beyond her property. The boys got even with her by tying firecrackers to an arrow and shooting it into the cook's open window on the third floor.

As I worked with all these younger people, I found their enthusiasm so contagious that I plunged into a display of astonishingly pompous editorials, fables, feature articles, parables and essays. I couldn't quite catch up to Jim with getting *everything* I wrote into print but I came pretty close to it. There were plenty of others besides myself filling *The Local's* columns with news and reminiscences. Novelist Barbara Rex had her own column for a while; Polly Brinley, queen of "Letters to the Editor Page" kept us fully aware of the essentials for neighborhood improvement; and Helen Moak wrote in her delicate style on the subjects of church history, public administration and mental health. Mike Von Moschzisker ran an informative column on political matters for a time, and Dr. John McClenahan frequently entertained us with his "Light and Lively" essays.

My greatest rival on *The Local* was Marion Rivinus—Mrs. E. Florens Rivinus. She was a little older than I and the author of several books. In 1966 she was honored as a Distinguished Daughter of Pennsylvania, and in 1967 won the Chestnut Hill Award for "her boundless feeling for our community, and her ability to kindle joy in others—Chestnut Hill's great lady and friend."

We vied with each other over who could get the most childhood memories of Chestnut Hill into the pages of *The Local*. Then we struck up a series of commentaries and replies in *The Local* which began with the following letters:

Dear Marion, [I wrote] As one Chestnut Hill woman to another you know I have a difficult assignment as a married woman. Each year I am forced to spend several weeks away from our beloved Hill, traveling among West Indian dream islands, and wandering through worlds of quiet elegance and charm as if each sun spot or fun spot was my own private estate. But there are plenty of ants in all this sugar and I'd like to send you a little of that raw material on which you could focus your wit and turn it into an article for *The Local*. Does this appeal to your fancy, your whim, your salty Attic wit? If so I'll jet it up to you from Grand Bahama, Grande Cayman, Rio Grande, Boca Grande, or Grande Terre. You can, naturally, always find me at the Hotel Splendide in any of these places. And for goodness' sake send me a copy of *The Local* when your article comes out, and tell me what's going on in Chestnut Hill.—Love, Mary.

Response:

Dear Mary, I sympathize deeply with your marital problems. For years I too had to desert Chestnut Hill for fishing in Norway, shooting in Scotland, and the tedious life on Waikiki Beach in Honolulu. To cap it

113

all we left dear Chestnut Hill each January for Palm Beach to remain until April. It was a terrible experience . . .

To get back to the pith of your letter. Why should I write an alluring travel talk about an unknown island when Chestnut Hill has so much more to offer? There's nothing novel about cocktail parties and dancing the Calypso, but the Hill has a very new social activity to offer—Shovel Visiting. It always snows on Fridays and by Sunday the local inhabitants have dug themselves out to the sidewalks. The snow is wet and heavy and much time has to be consumed resting on the shovel. Here is where the social part comes in. While pausing we visit. You have no idea what world decisions are made and local gossip imparted. While *your* brains are being stagnated *ours* are being alerted by brilliant conversation. I really feel for what you are missing but I await your next epistle with keen interest.—Love, Marion.

Response:

Dear Marion, Have just received *The Local*, and your article! What understanding! What Attic wit (why do you keep it in the attic?) What banter, whimsy, chaff and persiflage! Chestnut Hill can't do without you and your articles. They inspire me, so here is some more raw material: broken beer bottles and rubber tires on beaches, the heads of sharks and old rags caught in seaweed, a native washing his mule in the sea, orange peels and egg shells dotting the gently sloping sand, and the pungent smell of refuse in the air. Neat place for a refreshing swim. Will be keen to see what you can do with *these* ants in the sugar.— Love, Mary.

This sort of thing went on and off and on again for seven years until we decided to bury the hatchet which we did by bringing out a pamphlet called *Ants in the Sugar* and *Salt in the Attic*, illustrated with humorous drawings by Marion's daughter Betty. It contained all our vignettes as well as our Chestnut Hill-West Indian letters, and Editor-in-Chief Ellen wrote the following foreword:

When two of our village of Chestnut Hill's most formidable ladies picked the pages of *The Chestnut Hill Local* to sling their sugared and salted arrows at each other right over the editorial desk, it was with some reservations that I consented to act as referee. Were there not more pressing problems to employ the limited columns of a small community paper? Zoning battles, Main Street Fairs, archeological diggings on the Rex Avenue sewer, and the Generation Gap, Chestnut Hill style?

Somewhat to my chagrin I found their attic wits and peppery ant-ics were attracting more attention among our readers than a new neon sign on Germantown Avenue. Only recently a reader wrote plaintively that "a few more articles like those of Mmes. Bond and Rivinus and all wranglings are sighed away."

Those rollicking, crusading days are over, but *The Local* has managed to go on and on and thrive without us.

CHAPTER 9

1963–1966

PHILADELPHIA, MAINE AND the Caribbean now formed an equilateral triangle around my life, punctuated by Jim's roving spirit which took us to England, France or Switzerland, and, when in Maine, to Canada's Gaspé Peninsula, Grand Manan and Prince Edward Island. I visited South Carolina less frequently, and when in Charleston I now stayed with my cousins Emily and Ben Scott Whaley. Josephine Pinckney had died, as had DuBose Heyward and Hervey Allen. But Anne and Kershaw Fishburne were still at Pinopolis, although Anne wrote me, "I need a new pair of eyes and a new pair of ears." Sam Stoney also wrote to me. "Dear Coz," be began. "Prepare yourself for longevity. Three of our kin have recently died, one made it to the cover of *Time Magazine* and all were in their nineties. I can't face thirty more years of this." Both Sam and I were in our sixties and I took his last statement lightly, not realizing how seriously he had meant what he'd written. Ten years later he shot himself.

At home in Philadelphia the glamorous days of the Clark and Dilworth era were receding rapidly into infinity, the way railroad ties do when you watch them from an observation car's rear platform on a speeding train. Joe was now our senator and doing a good job in Washington. Dick, after losing his campaign for governor to William Scranton, was presiding over Philadelphia's Board of Education. Before he left the mayor's office he put me on the Advisory Board of Tinicum Marsh, a swampy area in South Philadelphia which came under the jurisdiction of the Recreation Department. Not many cities have a nature sanctuary of that size within city limits and under chairmanship of Allston Jenkins, Philadelphia's "Mr. Conservationist," the preserve became a popular recreation area and remains so today.

I found myself no longer active in politics but involved with other civic interests—the Free Library, Tinicum, editorial meetings of *The*

117

Chestnut Hill Local, and, of course, my writing. I wrote more and more articles about the West Indies and I told Jim I would soon have enough for a book that I intended to call *Far Afield in the Caribbean.* He was not particularly enthusiastic.

"You really haven't been very far afield, you know," he said.

"I have so!" I replied. "Turneffe may have been a run-of-the-mill episode in your roving life, but to me it was a soul-fulfilling experience. And how about Cozumel?"

"Cozumel! It was a tourist resort!"

"It wasn't when we were there."

"I admit that Turneffe was a bit off the beaten path, but up to now the *Ornis* expedition is really the only 'far afield' you've ever been on. Why not write that up?"

"I'll do just that!" I replied. "And I'll start at the very beginning— how you'd always wanted to go to Los Testigos and how it came about that you finally got there!"

Los Testigos is one of the many islands off the coast of Venezuela which mark the outposts of the continental shelf of South America. Some don't even show on North American maps, being of interest only to local fishermen and scientists—desert islands in truth, off in a corner of the Caribbean far from the usual sea-lanes and air routes. No wonder they were used as excellent hideaways for stolen booty in the old buccaneering days of Drake, Raleigh, Swan and Morgan.

After the buccaneers the scientists came. In 1682 William Dampier, an English navigator and explorer, landed on La Blanquilla and wrote up a description of it. In 1807, Lavayesse, a Frenchman, spent some time there. In 1859, Count Dalmas landed and collected but never published what he found. And in 1833, Richard Ludwig, the German geologist, visited all the islands but failed to find the guano deposits he was looking for—a much sought-after item during the 19th Century which had attracted seamen from as far away as the downeast coast of Maine.

At the turn of this century, Mr. William H. Phelps went down from the United States to seek his fortune and found it in Venezuela. Among his many other interests he began a vast ornithological project concentrating wholly on Venezuela. His great contribution was to pin down the precise ranges of Venezuelan birds, which meant the gigantic task of collecting on every mountain and island belonging to that country. A map of Venezuela in his *Lista de Las Aves de Venezuela* is dotted with numbered circles indicating more than 350 "collecting stations."

Jim had met Bill Phelps senior on several occasions at the American

118

Museum of Natural History in New York, and he had often said, "Why don't you come with us on one of our *Ornis* trips?" "I will," Jim would reply, "if you'll take me to Los Testigos." "Too far," was the usual answer.

Los Testigos was of special interest to Jim because of its proximity to the Lesser Antilles. With Grenada but forty miles away, this small group of islands posed the usual question about "fringe" islands—how strong was the nearby Antillean element? Years ago Jim had read a paper called A Naturalist on Desert Islands, by Percy Lowe, a British ornithologist of the early 20th century who reported having seen an owl and a hawk on Los Testigos. On several past expeditions the Phelpses had failed to locate either one, and doubted if they were there. At last they decided to give Jim a chance to take a look for them himself.

Like most successful expeditions ours was the result of pooled experiences, discussions, letters and chance meetings at natural history conferences in Basle, Boston, New York and Paris, all playing their part in setting a date for this particular expedition to six of the Venezuelan islands—Los Testigos being the second on our schedule. Could I handle it?

"If Mr. Phelps at eighty-four can handle it, I ought to be able to." This was my stand. It was one thing to have gone with Jim six years previously to the lonely lagoons and mangrove islands of Turneffe, but I was just that much older now. It would be quite another thing to become part of a seasoned group of explorer-scientists all younger than I (except for Bill Phelps, Sr.), on an expedition in the Phelpses' ketch the *Ornis*, over hundreds of miles of open Caribbean to "work" six desert islands or island groups strung out along the continental shelf of South America.

All my life I had been aware of looking younger than my years, sometimes a definite disadvantage that others found difficult to understand. But anyone over sixty knows full well that the cliché "you're only as old as you feel" is eradicated by two other clichés—"there's no fool like and old fool" who "bites off more than she can chew."

"Of course you can handle it," Jim reassured me as we sat under one of the flowered umbrellas on the terrace of The Mona Hotel, Jamaica. "You're a far better sailor than I am, the Phelpses know exactly what they're doing and they've taken along all sorts of wives on their *Ornis* expeditions."

"So I've heard," I murmured, recalling some cryptic remarks about one or two of these wives and their tiresome idiosyncrasies while aboard. I was quite capable of exhibiting some of my own: the need to be alone during some part of the day, and a violent aversion to drafts on the back of my neck. I just wished I had done this ten years before and couldn't help thinking too of the many stories I'd read dramatizing personality clashes among people cooped up together in the same boat. I also realized through some of Jim's early experiences that even with the best will in the world an expedition can be ruined if a single member becomes a serious liability through illness or sheer cussedness. But here was something I'd wanted to do all my life and I was determined to soft pedal my unusual lack of self-confidence.

At my suggestion we went down for a few days before the date set for meeting the Phelpses who lived in Caracas. "To get acclimated," I told Jim, who knew as well as I did about that first bout of inertia which follows a too rapid change from chilly weather to tropical heat. "Good idea," was Jim's response. We flew down on the *Brittania*, a BOAC jet, where the stewards wore pink hunting coats to serve us at 20,000 feet in midair. Equally ridiculous to my mind was the elaborate luncheon of asparagus soup, champagne, lobster and mayonnaise, lamb cutlets (chops, to me), broccoli, candied sweet potatoes—all from a small tea-wagon which fitted neatly into the narrow aisle. Then came white or red wine, a bowl of salad, and, for dessert, red-colored canned pears in jelly with whipped cream, and a bone tooth-pick, such as my father used to use.

Across the aisle was someone familiar but I couldn't put a name to her until we were approaching Montego Bay. Of course—It was Liz Taylor, looking hot and sweaty and supposedly suffering from a broken leg. Just before landing she made her way with apparent ease to the toilet, returning with one leg bound up in gauze from knee to ankle. I didn't want to miss her debarkation and, except for me, she was the last to leave the plane. A secretary carried her mink coat and she hobbled down the gangway wearing just the right thing for a broken leg—a hobble skirt and high-heeled shoes. Eddie Fisher was in attendance and a helicopter waited nearby. The dear girl managed with crutches to reach the copter, but gallantly set the crutches aside to allow herself to be helped into a side-saddle position on the hood for the camera men.

With Miss Taylor safely on her way, Jim and I checked into the Mona Hotel which we liked because of its proximity to the Reservoir which sometimes produced ducks, grebes, coots, and, in the woodsy section, unseen but heard, the mysterious, secret notes of the white-bellied dove. It was always a scorching hot walk which I welcomed, and after a couple of days of warm Jamaica weather we were ready for Caracas.

At the La Guaira airport, the Venezuelan customs officer took a long time climbing our family tree and writing down the names of our parents and grandparents. They stamped the Venezuelan seal on everything we owned, and by the time we reached our hotel we were shaken and weak from our ride. Every turn in the road was a crisis, the driver a wild barbarian constantly turning his head around and yelling good-naturedly to us that everything in Caracas was "muy cara."

We found a sweet welcoming note from Kathy Phelps, William Phelps' dynamic daughter-in-law, and fell into our beds to be awakened by her at 7:45 A.M. the next morning. After the amenities were over, her first question was—"Are you *well?* Is Jim *well?*" confirming Jim's remark that the Phelpses knew what they were doing. In fact, from that moment on I knew that Kathy was in charge.

She came for us at the hotel and we were ready, our cruise clothes in two carryalls. We hadn't seen Kathy since last year in Paris where I had found it easy to fall in with her enthusiasms. Her interests were wide, her accomplishments varied, her published series of Venezuelan birds painted with great delicacy and accuracy. During the cruise, her passion for underwater spear-fishing provided us daily with fresh lobster and fish.

Bill, Jr. was at the house when we arrived and it was good to see him—a large man, powerful, tremendously likable and hospitable. In fact, we were overcome with their hospitality. And if I wasn't excited enough already, just being there in their house would have been enough. The house itself was beautiful—white plaster built around a square patio open to the sky. You walked in the front door to a tiled rotunda with pale yellow walls and black doors leading to a powder room, closets and a bathroom. On the right, through an open doorway to the dining room, you saw white filmy curtains billowing from the windows between heavy gold draperies. Opposite was the formal drawing room, the motif in cool, soft greens and magnificent flower arrangements on side tables. They "lived" in the patio, the court overlooking the garden through four high arched iron-grilles. Against one wall were the obvious signs of thorough preparations for the expedition: machetes, guns, diving gear, underwater spears for catching fish all stacked against a table laden with canteens, cameras, boxes of cartridges and bird-skinning equipment. Also, Kathy's guitar. I noticed our duffel placed next to a pile of sleeping bags.

We all sat down in comfortable chintz-covered chairs facing the garden. Vines had been trained against a wall and at intervals hanging baskets dripped with orchids. Among the vines in the iron grilles, sugar-water vials attracted dozens of humming-birds. We found ourselves peering through a shimmering screen of at least fourteen varieties to the

121

lower garden where a huge tree threw a lacy shadow-pattern on closely-clipped green grass.

Kathy began to give us a rundown of our plans. Bill Phelps Sr. was already on board the *Ornis*, waiting for us ninety miles away on Isla de Margarita. He, with two captains and crew, had gone ahead some days before. That night at ten o'clock Dillon Ripley, director of the Peabody Museum at Yale (later, secretary of the Smithsonian Institution) and his wife Mary, were due from New York at La Guaira airport. All of us would spend the night "*chez* Phelps" as Kathy put it, at their beach house a few miles outside La Guaira. Early in the morning we would fly the ninety miles to Margarita and join the *Ornis*.

Suddenly the telephone rang. Bill got up to answer it. Kathy, watching his face said, "It's Father! Calling from Margarita." She looked worried. Still watching Bill, who was speaking Spanish, she added, "One of the *Ornis*'s engines has gone on the blink."

The conversation continued. It was a breathless moment. Was the entire expedition to be cancelled?

"But the Bonds are here," Bill said in English. "And the Ripleys are arriving tonight. We can't let these people down when they've come so far."

The discussion continued in Spanish. Kathy's face was my only clue to what would be decided. Her face suddenly cleared. Bill hung up and said, "Father finally consented. He said okay, but bring along an extra sail and we'll take a chance."

Bill left at once to round up the extra sail. By late afternoon he returned, and we all drove up the mountain to their weekend "cottage," an enchanting little thatched-roof white plaster building perched on a knoll. Kathy took me off for a little walk, past the greenhouse to a ravine full of jungly growth, sprawling roots, tree ferns, and, at the end, a bit of a climb. I began to smile. A little test of my agility? Whether I could or could not get in and out of boats? I hoped my performance settled any of her private fears. Unforgettable was the sunset from the top of that mountain and, after dark, watching the lights come out in the sprawling city of Caracas below. It looked like a bowl of glittering jewels six miles long in a valley of purple velvet.

Down again into the stifling city. No street signs. You simply had to know your way around. Then the soft comfort and relaxation in the little beach house where we had a light supper under almond trees in the small tropical garden with the roar of the surf below us. Later, when Jim went to bed and the Phelpses drove off to meet the Ripleys at the airport, I slipped out and took a nyad swim in the little salt pool, air and water too deliciously balmy for words, and thought over the events of the day.

Venezuela was disturbing and unlovable. One was aware of the undercurrent of revolt and violence. The government arbitrarily seized people's land and they often retaliated by setting fire to the forests. Whole mountainsides had been burned this year. That very afternoon a policeman had been shot and killed. We had heard the shots. Kathy told us that many of the servants were spies and I had noticed, with shock, that if one of us wished to walk in their garden, an iron gate on the patio had to be unlocked, and locked up again, on our return. We also learned that just ten days before, the *Ornis* had been stripped at her berth at the Yacht Club—blankets, bedding, supplies and sailing gear all had to be hurriedly replaced. This added complication only made it clearer to us how generous and hospitable were our hosts and hostess.

The Ripley's plane was late and Jim and I did not see them until at breakfast the next morning. Mary R. (I was to become Mary B.) carried a large sack containing an enormous piece of needlepoint. She was used to accompanying her husband on many expeditions even as far afield as New Guinea—occasions when a scientist's wife is often "on her own" for untold hours back at camp. She called the needlepoint her "occupational therapy."

We were all very glad to see each other, and had much to talk about on the flight in a tiny plane to Isla de Margarita. There we were met at the airport by Mr. Phelps, the two captains, and the crew of the *Ornis*. It was a short drive to Porlamar where I thrilled at my first sight of the *Ornis* lying offshore. She was sixty-five feet of white, immaculate, streamlined loveliness, especially designed by the Phelpses for their expeditions among the islands. Her outstanding feature was her roomy, glass-enclosed cabin on the main deck amidship where seven or eight people could be seated and keep an eye on whatever was going on inside or outside. Glass louvres at the windows regulated the flow of air, and the dining table pulled out from a wall like an accordion in front of a couch which seated three people comfortably. Folding chairs were set up opposite and whoever sat at the end of the table near the hatch helped to pass plates and platters handed up from the galley below. After the meal was over the table was pushed back out of the way and the folding chairs stowed in a corner. This left the couch and several cushioned chairs to sit on, the latter heavy enough to remain stable in rough weather. How often were we to sit around that hospitable cabin and sink down gratefully into soft cushions after a hot, rugged day on shore!

Getting us and our belongings on board was handled with despatch.

123

It took three round trips of the *Ornis Jr.* to complete the job. According to law, all Venezuelan ships were required to carry a Venezuelan captain. The *Ornis* employed another as well; Captain Flotman, a North American of Dutch extraction who had been with the Phelpses for many years. Antonio was the youngest member of the crew, a dark, handsome young man with a brilliant smile and somewhat the look of a Saracen. He could speak no English but was very quick, and reminded me of one of my Charleston cousins.

When satisfied that nothing had been forgotten, we pulled anchor and without delay headed into the trades for our first island, *Los Frailes* (The Friars). As soon as we were at sea Kathy called Mary R. and me below. A small passage ran between two cabins, each with a single bunk and a tiny closet. At the end was what Kathy called "The Bridal Suite," complete with two bunks and its own private bath.

"We'll draw lots," she explained briskly," to see whether the Bonds or the Ripleys get the bridal suite first. Halfway along you'll change over."

By the grace of the gods the Bonds got it first and Jim could at least be in privacy for his first bouts of seasickness which, as he knew, he would get over in a day or two, and did.

"And now there are two things that must be clearly understood," Kathy went on. "Number one—water. Water is priceless on a boat and nobody must be allowed to waste it!" She opened the door to "the head" and showed us how to use the basin spigots sparingly. "Second—somebody's got to be in command, which means that when you're told to do something in a hurry, you do it."

Mary R. and I exchanged smiles. It was clear to us both that our commanding officer was Kathy.

Landing was easy at *Los Frailes* but the heat on the beach was like a blast from an open furnace. I was dismayed by the height of the cactus. Thickets fifteen feet high trapped and distilled the sun's rays and made breathing hard work. But the men did return with lizards, birds, and shells lacking in the collections at the Peabody Museum (Dillon's concern) and the Philadelphia Academy of Natural Sciences.

That evening we sat in the stern over our drinks with the Venezuelan flag fluttering behind us. Pelicans fed in the blue dusk and frigate birds circled overhead. We were all content, at least it looked that way. On the other hand, here were four prominent naturalists—and scientists, like artists, take strong personal pride in their theories and the way in which they tackle their jobs. Would there be any serious clashes?

Captain Flotman was also our chef and gave us for supper that night pork chops, mashed potatoes, peas, bread and huge stewed strawberries. Afterwards we sat in deep chairs in the main cabin and wrote up our notes. Mary R. tackled her tapestry and I was amused to hear the four men refer to whatever birds came into the conversation by their Latin names! Everyone turned in early, Jim and I luxurious in the bridal suite, Mary R. and Kathy in the port and starboard cabins, Bill Jr. and Dillon on air mattresses on the main cabin floor and Bill Sr. on the couch made up by Antonio into a bed.

No one got more than a few snatches of sleep, for the *Ornis* rolled all night long. At five A.M. the vibration of the engines and the forward thrust of the ketch told me we were on our way—at last—to *Los Testigos*! But the next five hours spent in covering the forty miles were among the most wretched in my life. Jim was violently seasick the whole way. I never saw anything like it. How could he possibly be fit to go ashore? Were all our hopes and plans to end in nothing but disappointment? I tried to bring him some orange juice from the galley. The trip there and back was like a workout in a gymnasium and the glass but half full when I managed to pass it to him. He waved it away and said heroically, "Don't forget—all the discomforts on a trip like this are forgotten when it's over. The cream rises to the top and that's what you remember."

At ten o'clock we dropped anchor in the lee of Los Testigos and the sudden calm and silence were like a benediction. To my utter astonishment Jim bounced back like a rubber ball! After a bottle of beer, of all things, and his only breakfast, he was raring to go. In fact all of us were hyped up pretty thoroughly. I was certainly beside myself with excitement.

We assembled in the main cabin to await our turn to be taken ashore in the *Ornis Jr.*, a dory with an outboard motor. Luis and Antonio already had it over the side at the bottom of the ladder. Dillon wore an orange shirt and white duck hat, camera and binoculars slung around his neck. Mary R. wore shorts of the same color—a good distinguishing mark on a dazzling beach a mile away. Kathy wore a blue straw hat and protected her camera and binoculars inside a cellophane bag tied around her neck. Bill Jr., in boots and duck hat, was equipped with a gun, machete, canteen and camera, and when Jim appeared Kathy's face was a study.

"Oh, *Jim!*" she exclaimed. "All the rest of us are ready to go ashore!"

"So am I," he said, and I laughed. Jim wore his usual long twill trousers, long sleeved cotton shirt and no hat. He never carried binoculars or took photographs. Besides his gun all he had today was a handkerchief and a bottle of insect repellant in his pocket.

I shook my head slowly. "It's no use, Kathy. But don't worry—cactus, snakes, swamps, and hot sun—he's been the despair of all his doctor friends for years. They think he should be dead fifty times by now. He just seems to get by."

At the end of that day tension raised its threatening head. Los Testigos was not an inviting island and the morning's work was disappointing. Everyone returned to the *Ornis* hot and tired. Even our anchorage was uncomfortable until Captain Flotman nosed us around a point to a heavenly cove where a curving beach of pink sand threw loving arms around mint green shallows superb for swimming. There was a fresh breeze, and on the sand hundreds of laughing gulls facing into it all at the same angle. Pelicans sat placidly off shore and I would have been happy to settle here for the duration. But not a bit of it. We were not engaged in a casual outing on a pleasure yacht but involved in a tightly planned scientific expedition. And directly after lunch everyone, including Bill, Sr., went ashore again. Jim and Dillon presented a ludicrous sight, both men walking off wearing nothing but sneakers and swim trunks, and carrying guns. I associated Jim and guns with hunting attire. But again nothing of importance was found in the afternoon and everyone except Jim was eager to move on to the other islands. Especially, as Kathy pointed out, what with time, fuel and water being limited, Los Roques, the "Playground of the Gods," promised to be more rewarding.

"It depends on what you call rewarding," Jim told me as we changed our clothes for the evening. "I'm not looking for a playground of the gods. I'm trying to find out how much Antillean element, if any, is found on these islands, and now that we're actually on the spot I'd like to stay a week and work this island thoroughly."

After supper that night we held a pow-wow around a bonfire on shore. The stars came out—big, bright, glowing things, hot and alive. Everyone was polite. Underneath was tension. It was interesting to listen to pros and cons, never heated but reserved, concise and reasonable with intervals of pregnant silence.

At last Bill Sr. broke the silence and said, "After all, wasn't *Testigos* one of the primary objectives of this expedition? We'll stay as long as Jim wants to stay."

This put it up to Jim and they reached a compromise to stay for one more full day's work. Alas, that too drew a blank. Jim was extremely disappointed but acknowledged he was satisfied that nothing more of interest could be found on *Los Testigos*. His notes summed up the story: "Subspecies not represented in the Academy's collection obtained here, but no records of scientific import. Record of hawk or owl discounted."

Just before dawn, when it's supposed to be less windy, we sailed off on an eight hour run to *Los Hermanos*, the "Seven Brothers." And that night I woke up with a raging sore throat and a throbbing ear. A cold? A strange virus? What was the matter with me? Was I to become one of those lame ducks that wives gossip about? Both discomforts mysteriously disappeared when I got on deck, and I soon forgot all about them.

Looking back now after twenty-six years, I can see that I had approached this expedition from the first without my usual self-confidence. Nor did I know that the subsequent attacks of sore throat and earache were caused by my being allergic to certain sea food, a mainstay of our menu throughout the cruise. Although mystified by recurrent attacks, I was determined to enjoy every aspect of this experience, however fast and furious the program was. We were among islands lost in time and lonely in space—*Los Hermanos*, *Orchila*, *La Blanquilla* and the magnificent *Los Roques* archipelago—the latter some twenty by thirty miles in area and dotted with numerous islets bearing witness to British sea-dog influence. Northeast Cay, for example, became *Nordisqui* and Long Key, *Lanqui*. We especially enjoyed *Yonqui*—from downeast Maine? And *Uisqui*—Dewar's White Label? There can scarcely be any island laboratories more remote than those of Venezuela. We saw, we came, we conquered and made no impression on them whatsoever, our footprints in the sand vanishing under the trade winds moments after we had sailed away.

At *Los Hermanos* all was hatred and jealousy, violence and grandeur! Each of the "Seven Brothers" presented a classic example of the immovable body meeting the irresistible force—each in his own way a grim gray fortress rearing up from the horizon against a golden dawn, standing firm and obstinate against the Atlantic Ocean's crashing combers attacking their guano-mantled crags. Under a skyful of screaming terns, the *Ornis* passed them by, all of us on board caught up in the wild windy mood of attack and defense. Landing was out of the question. The mountainous waves were sucked into the caves and spewed out again with force and fury. All we could do was to sail past them disconsolately while high overhead a peregrine falcon, as if to mock our human limitations, slid toward the sea on an edge of wind.

Even the *Ornis* was glad to show her heels to that hostile group—and how she ran before the wind! Heading due west with the trades behind us we covered the thirty miles to *La Blanquilla* in record time, stopping just once in the lee of *Orchila* for a decent breakfast of scrambled eggs, bacon, toast, coffee and marmalade. Kathy told us wild stories of this Sodom and Gomorrah desert island, once the playground of a bygone dictator who built a summer palace here, brought trees, shrubs and flowers from the mainland (they died of course) and was reported to have invited twenty chorus girls for a visit, providing them with lovely bathing suits which dissolved in salt water. He then amused himself by chasing his flock of nymphs around the beach in his electrified beach-mobile . . .

And that unforgettable afternoon at *La Blanquilla*! As we ran along its coast line I picked out a beautiful little cove which I intended to visit alone, lie in the sun, and burn out of me what I still considered a kind of cold. Once ashore all the others went off in different directions, and I told Jim of my plans. Wearing a wide-brimmed hat, bathing suit and beach jacket, I set forth against the scorching wild wind which did not gust but just blew steadily. I could almost lean against it, and could hardly wait for a dip in the clear green shallows of what looked like heaven from the boat and turned out to be a veritable hell! Once below the lip of the steep coral bank there was no air, no wind, nothing but *heat*. I flung off my jacket and rushed into the water, gasped at its hellish temperature and struggled out, exhausted, infuriated and almost in tears. I struggled up the coral, made my way back to where Bill Sr. was sitting alone in the shade of some palms, his legs crossed in a Buddha-like position, and tried to calm down.

But something fierce was building up in me, and when I awoke the following morning in my tiny port cabin (we had by now "changed over" with the Ripleys) I was in a rebellious mood, angry over my physical limitations, sorry for myself, and not fit for human society. So, after all, I had bitten off more than I could chew, and told Jim I needed a day off. He understood, everybody understood, and they all went ashore, including Bill Sr., leaving me alone on board with the two captains who also needed a rest. A rest? I'd forgotten how to rest. I lay on my bunk all morning, sweating, desperate, trapped and off base, raging against being one of the eleven humans enclosed on a sixty-five foot ketch and cut off from the flow of life everywhere else on earth. Every episode, small or large, was magnified in our tight little world out of proportion to its actual importance. Perhaps the others felt this way too but were handling it better than I. I was failing. I couldn't conform and my vanity was hurt. What *could* I do? what could I *think*? I wanted to be where I was more than anywhere else but I couldn't handle it. Jim was in his element. How could I get back on the beam?

I began to think about the Phelpses' hospitality and all the trouble they had taken over this expedition. I focused on what I liked about Kathy and each of the others and, like a drifting cloud, the rhythm of a sonnet's iambic-pentameter floated through my mind . . . "The plowman homeward plods his weary way" turned into "The queenly *Ornis,* anchored, stands serene/ In mint-green waters sheltered by the reef!'". That's what I'd do! And I did—spending the whole afternoon lying on that bunk blessedly absorbed in shaping up for Bill Sr. three four-line stanzas with a rhyming couplet at the end. So I wasn't useless after all!

Kathy, with her flair for the dramatic, put me on stage during the cocktail hour and with the help of Dillon's flashlight I read my sonnet aloud. It wasn't much of a sonnet but Bill Sr. was pleased and said, "Never before has anyone written me a poem." I began to purr inside and in such manner I got my second wind for the latter half of the expedition at *Los Roques.*

Kathy of course was right. *Los Roques* was not only an Olympian playground for those who loved snorkeling and underwater fishing, but rewarding even for the scientists. In *Espenqui* they discovered a nesting colony of black noddys, the first seen in the Caribbean for nearly a century. No earth-shaking news that would change the course of biological thought, no headliner on the order of astronauts stepping out on the moon, or being "the first person to walk alone in space," but just another satisfying expedition of four naturalists devoted to their profession. Of such is the kingdom of science.

What the rest of us did in *Los Roques* I have written up elsewhere in detail (*To James Bond with Love,* Sutter House, pages 130–152) and when on our last night aboard I asked Jim how he felt about the whole expedition, he said, "Frankly I'm disappointed in what it's yielded in land birds. But Kathy was right. *Los Roques* more than made up for it. I confess I have always neglected pelagic species. Oceanic birds obey different zoögeographic rules from land birds, and aren't useful to the zoögeographer. But in the last few days I've learned more about sea birds than in all my West Indian trips put together."

Nor had he done so badly. He brought back ten new birds to the Academy's collection.

A lemon colored dawn crept around the purple headlands of the Venezuela coast when at last the *Ornis* snuggled into her berth at La Guaira's marina. It was all I could do to leave her! I looked back at her stream-lined loveliness, sentimental about everything: Bill Sr. in his nook in the main cabin reading his paperbacks; the pink plastic cloth Antonio battened down on top of the cabin when we lunched on board— always rice, lobster, conch or fresh fish, rows of tomatoes, hard-boiled eggs, pickles, canned fruit, or melons or apples for dessert; the crew's table forward beyond the galley where Jim and Dillon spent whole afternoons skinning birds; even the mess in the morning when the three men got up in the main cabin; Kathy's guitar case (we both played it once or twice); guns, bags of ammunition, trays with bottles of arsenic, scalpels and cotton for skinning specimens; the clutter on the poop deck of snorkels and fish guns; the bathing-suits, clusters of orchids; large fragments of Indian relics; jars of strange jelly fish and lizards in alcohol; shells from each island carefully labelled and dated; and snails cleaned out before being confined to Dillon's inexhaustible supply of airtight cellophane bags. Already the discomforts of cramped quarters were beginning to fade, but never to be forgotten were the soft evenings in the stern, the stories told, the labyrinth of water-ways on some of the islands, and the deep blue of the Caribbean Sea. Already the cream was rising to the top.

Chapter 10

1966–1972

Although born and bred a Philadelphian, it was clear that Jim's life was not to follow the conventional pattern of most of his contemporaries. He went his own way, preferring a low profile and, when possible, invisibility. To quote Wordsworth, he was a man "voyaging through strange seas alone." Perhaps we should not have then been too surprised when an undreamed of intrusion thrust its way into his private life like a bolt out of the blue. This came in the form of a review in the *London Sunday Times* of the just published third edition of his field guide *Birds of the West Indies*.

WRONG MAN

"Image" is the new nauseating word. I can barely bring myself to write that James Bond, like practically every one else mentioned in the newspapers these days, is trying to establish a new image of himself.

To show maybe that his life is not all sadomasochism, Smith and Wessons, and *écrivisse*-tails in a white wine and brandy sauce, Bond has revealed himself as a bird watcher: and I shouldn't be a bit surprised if his *Birds of the West Indies*, which comes from Collins tomorrow, doesn't place him ornithologically speaking well above Mr. Wolf Mankowitz, but somewhere below Earl Grey of Falloden, W.H. Hudson, Lord Alanbrooke and the people who feed the pigeons in Trafalgar Square.

As the subject of West Indian birds is not without its sensational aspects, one must hope that Mr. Bond has seen fit to preserve a decent discretion, particularly in his treatment of the nuptual plumage of the copper-rumped humming bird (Amazilia tobaci) and the private life of the scaly-breasted thrasher.

P.S. Terrible mistake! I now find that the author of *Birds of the West Indies* is a different James Bond, Curator at the Academy of Natural Sciences, Philadelphia, and a top banana in ornithology. You may have complete confidence in this Mr. Bond who knows all about species, habitat, nidification and the reversible outer-toe of the osprey or fish-hawk.

We couldn't make head nor tail of it. Why this facetious approach to the rarely hilarious profession of ornithology? Shock after shock followed. By chance, our old friend Jackson Marshall, overseas representative of Collins whom we frequently saw in the Caribbean, happened to be in New York at the time. Through a telephone conversation he explained that an English writer, Ian Fleming, had written several detective thrillers and had hit on the name James Bond for his secret agent. It was the first time we'd heard of Ian Fleming or of his 007 books.

Number two shock came through a copy of *Rogue Magazine* featuring an article with a huge picture of Ian Fleming under the category "Personality" which ran: "A tour with the creator of James Bond, *Goldfinger*, and the insidious *Dr. No*, as he seeks sin, Chicago style." I read the interview, passed over some sensational fold-outs and reached the following paragraph:

"My first book," Fleming admitted, "was a lark to write. I knew a bit about gambling and about the secret service and thought it would be jolly to combine them. There really is a James Bond, you know. I had a copy of his *Birds of the West Indies*, and when casting about for a natural sounding name for my hero I recalled the guide and lifted the author's name outright."

What prompted him to make this admission? Did he think that nobody would pick this up, that the kind of people who read *Rogue* didn't go in for nature field guides—and the reverse?

Shock number three was an interview published in *The New Yorker*, again under the heading "Bond's Creator" (which began to annoy me as being a bit blasphemous). Fleming was quoted as saying "I wanted 007 to be an extremely uninteresting man to whom things happened. One of the Bibles of my youth was *Birds of the West Indies* by James Bond and I thought, by God that's the dullest name I ever heard, so I appropriated it. Now the dullest name in the world has become an exciting one."

Ruth Seltzer, in her *Evening Bulletin* social column, was the first to call local attention to this dastardly theft, using the title of her article, "Will the Real James Bond Please Stand Up?" At the same time *The Chestnut Hill Local* used the heading "A Case of Double Identity" and presently Pete Martin, formerly with the Curtis Publishing Company, then writing for the *Sunday Bulletin*, came out to 721 Davidson Road for an interview with James Bond, adding it to his collection of *Pete*

Martin Calls On—a diverting book about more and less distinguished people. He was pleased to find certain similarities between 007 and Philadelphia's James Bond: both were interested in guns and the seriousness of making a good martini. The latter should be stirred, not shaken.

By this time I was reading all the 007 books published to date and was forcibly struck by a marked similarity of several West Indian bars, waterfronts, personalities, even incidents described by Fleming, to those Jim had related to me as his own experiences. I felt that Jim was being shadowed in a surreptitious way and decided to write to Mr. Fleming. I sent off my letter to his publishers, hoping the letterhead would give him a shock.

Feb. 1, 1961

Dear Mr. Fleming,

It was inevitable that we should catch up with you! First, the review in the London *Sunday Times* of my husband's new *Birds of the West Indies* revealed the existence of James Bond, British Agent.

Second, our friend Charles Chaplin of Haverford, Pa., and a friend of your brother Peter, gave us a copy of *Dr. No,* which explained the rest.

I read further stories about JBBA and became convinced that you must have been following JB *authenticus* around the West Indies, and picking up some of his adventures. It came to him as a surprise when we discovered in an interview published in *Rogue* magazine, that you had brazenly taken the name of a real human being for your rascal! And after reading *Dr. No,* my JB thought you'd been to Dirty Dick's in Nassau and talked with Old Farrington and got from him the story about the "Priscilla" and a wild trip about Jim's collecting parrots on Abaco. That was the time he spent several nights in a cave full of bats to get away from the mosquitoes.

As a rule truth is stranger than fiction but your JBBA proves this isn't necessarily so! Just don't let 007 marry—certainly not until he's 55!

This is a hurried letter because we're getting off to Yucatan and Cozumel this afternoon, thence back to Nassau where we'll spend a few days with the Chaplins.

I tell my JB he could sue you for defamation of character but he regards the whole thing as a joke.

Sincerely yours,

Mary Wickham Bond

A few months later he wrote me as follows:

4 *Old Mitre Street*
Fleet Street, London, E.C.4
20th June, 1961

Dear Mrs. James Bond,

I don't know where to begin to ask your forgiveness for my very tardy acknowledgment to your letter of February 1st.

I received it in Jamaica and since I was almost on the way to Nassau I decided to telephone the Chaplins on my arrival and get in touch with you and your husband.

Unfortunately I could get no reply from their telephone number and I again put your letter aside. Then, when I got back to England in March, I proceeded to have a swift heart attack which laid me out until now, and it is only to-day that your letter is again before me and the blackest of consciences is sitting on my shoulder.

I will confess at once that your husband has every reason to sue me in every possible position and for practically every kind of libel in the book, for I will now confess the damnable truth.

I have a small house which I built in Oracabessa in Jamaica just after the war, and some ten years ago, a confirmed bachelor on the eve of marriage, I decided to take my mind off the dreadful prospect by writing a thriller.

I was determined that my secret agent should be as anonymous a personality as possible. Even his name should be the very reverse of the kind of "Peregrine Carruthers" whom one meets in this type of fiction.

At that time one of my bibles was, and still is, *Birds of the West Indies* by James Bond, and it struck me that this name, brief, unromantic and yet very masculine, was just what I needed and so James Bond II was born, and started off on the career that, I must confess, has been meteoric, culminating with his choice by your President as his favourite thriller hero (see *Life* of March 17th).

So there is my dreadful confession together with limitless apologies and thanks for the fun and fame I have had from the most extraordinary chance choice of so many years ago.

In return I can only offer your James Bond unlimited use of the name Ian Fleming for any purpose he may think fit. Perhaps one day he will discover some particularly horrible species of bird which he would like to christen in an insulting fashion. That might be a way of getting his own back!

Anyway I send you both my most affectionate regards and good wishes, and should you ever return to Jamaica I would be very happy indeed to lend you my house for a week or so, so that you may inspect in comfort, the shrine where the second James Bond was born.

Yours sincerely,

(*By hand*)   *Ian Fleming*

Our friends bombarded us with phone calls and letters. "Sue him!" they cried. What was the point? Libel often made things only worse. Far more satisfying would be to confront Mr. Ian Fleming with the real James Bond. How to go about it? I knew Jim would do nothing but go on wincing and building up resentment at this intrusion into his own quiet life, as well as becoming disgusted when people slapped him on the back and winked slyly as if to say "You old lecher, you!" Also I felt there was something arrogant about Fleming's off-handed way of not only "lifting the name outright" but admitting it. Was there by any chance a touch of that well-known superiority of certain types of Englishmen towards Americans? Well, I wasn't going to have any of that, and even if Jim thought he could brush off the whole situation with a shrug I could not. A strange protective sense sprang up in me, a feeling I'd never had before towards anyone. Maternal perhaps. Never having had children of my own, that beautiful but dangerous instinct was a weak one with me. Even as a child I had never loved my dolls, glad that they got sick all the time and had to be kept in bed and out of my way. This did not mean I regarded Jim as a child, but it did imply that I wanted to protect his good name, his *amour propre*, and his strong sense of personal dignity. I was determined to see Ian Fleming's face when they met and my instinct for this meeting was correct: I got my pound of flesh but not immediately.

We went about our usual pattern of West Indies in winter and Maine in the summer. New 007 books came out and Hollywood got hold of them, overemphasizing the girlie-girlie angle. Then the powerful attraction of dollars began to propel the legend into the orbit of imaginative merchandizing. On the financial page of the *New York Herald Tribune* an article listed many items of killing, financially speaking, out of which hundreds of merchants hoped to make use of the magic number: "007 toiletries, whiskies, vodka, toys, trench coats, swim trunks began to pounce cat-like on the American market, entrapping the unwary male by spending money to dress, smell, and play at being Fleming's audacious spy."

The *New York Times* published a report from Paris "that James Bond has just entered the most frightening phase of his unpredictable career as Secret Agent 007. He is now selling bathrobes, raincoats, jewelry, dolls, gold lingerie and sheets. More than 3500 stores in France have obtained permission to use this prolific label."

From London came the news of plans to market a toy attaché case, plastic dagger, decoding machine and searchproof lock which, if tampered with, triggered a cap-firing device. There was also an adorable little automobile fitted with secret buttons which, when pushed, tossed the rider out of the car, raised a metal sheet behind the rear window to prevent being shot from behind, and ejected spikes from its wheels to attack any other car that came too close. One of these little toys is in the Rare Book Department of the Free Library of Philadelphia, Logan Square, in the Bondiana collection, along with a splendid bottle of 007 vodka, the label in red, black and gold, plus a plastic automatic pistol as a dispenser at the top.

As for ourselves, wherever we went all sorts of off-the-beam incidents happened. At a party in Philadelphia a lady rushed up to Jim and said, "Oh, Mr. Bond! I did enjoy so much your 'Dr. No!'" In Antigua, a taxi-driver said, "You gib me plenty sleepless nights, suh!" In Barbados a native lad dragged a friend up to Jim and asked, "Are you really James Bond?" Jim replied yes, and the boy nodded to his friend. "Didn't I tell you?" A little waitress at our hotel in Grenada handed Jim the menu and whispered in a Jacqueline Kennedy voice, "Are you really James Bond?" He nodded and once more I couldn't help trying to straighten things out by asking where she had first heard about James Bond. She said she had a book with the name of James Bond on it in big letters. I suggested there must have been other names on the cover but she shook her head, admitted she hadn't read it yet and that she hadn't really been interested. "But," with a fond look at Jim, "I am now!" I didn't mind this sort of thing, but when soft female voices called up, at two or three A.M. at Davidson Road, asking "Is James there?" I objected strongly. At first I'd say "Who's calling?" and might receive the reply "I think he'll know," or something equally silly. I finally put an end to such conversations by answering sharply, "Yes, James is here but this is a Pussy Galore and he's busy now."

One summer on board a liner to Southampton while looking over the passenger list on a bulletin board, a fellow passenger turned to us chuckling. "Whaddya know? James Bond's on board!" The name is invariably spoken in a whisper. And at Kingston, Jamaica, the customs' official boggled at the name on the baggage tags, looked up at Jim, the same type as Sean Connery (but far more handsome) and asked, "Anything to declare suh?" Jim answered, "No."

"No cigarettes? No liquor?"

"No."

Smiling ever so slightly, the officer then asked, "No firearms, suh?" Jim also smiled, "No, and if I had," he patted himself briskly under his arm where 007 carries his gun, "It wouldn't be in my suitcase, would it?"

Ian Fleming was delighted with these stories. And now as I look back twenty years later on that February day in 1964, when for the first and only time Ian Fleming met James Bond, I realize how dramatic it was. Just getting Jim into the picture had required a bit of wifely and extremely feminine plotting. But at least here we were, driving between the pink plaster gate-posts at Golden Eye up to the bungalow where we stopped behind a big Canadian Broadcasting Company's truck. A large black woman came out from the kitchen door as Jim stepped from the car and said, "Is Mr. Fleming at home?" She replied, "Yes, suh. Who shall I say is calling suh?"

"Mr. and Mrs. James Bond," Jim replied firmly.

A look of astonishment and shock went over her face. She turned and ran back into the house as if she'd seen a Zombie. Moments later Fleming appeared and here it was—Fleming and Bond *viz-a-vis*! The two men regarded each other for the fraction of a second and I held my breath. It was a kind of holy ghost situation. There Jim stood solid, real, a person both unconventional but always "correct," and there stood Fleming, his brow beaded with perspiration, his fair hair damp and curling British fashion behind his ears. And there, too, was the invisible but strong personality of 007 between them. Then Fleming put out his hand in quick, warm hospitality, his voice apologetic when he spoke about "all this bother I've made for you!" Something in me let go. It was going to be all right. I felt I was getting back "some of our own," as he had put it in his letter to me. Fleming had capitulated completely.

"The hell of it is I'm in the middle of a TV interview. But come in." Turning to me, he added, "You haven't come to threaten me with a libel suit, have you?"

"Oh no," I replied airily. "We just wanted to see where the second James Bond was born."

Inside the main room was a confusion of cables, cameras, sound equipment, spotlights and four impatient TV operators. Fleming dramatically flung out his arms and exclaimed "This is a bonanza for CBC! I never saw the man before in my life but here he is—the real James Bond stepping into the picture!" And to Jim, "This will sell even more of your books and mine!"

The cameras and sound trucks followed us to the terrace and whoever had written the script for the next couple of hours hadn't missed a trick. A lot of birds were flying about and Fleming, well-known for never letting a chance for a bit of show business to go by, asked Jim, "What kind of birds are they?" After all, couldn't any handsome stranger drop in and pass himself off as James Bond?

"Cave swallows," was Jim's matter-of-fact reply. "A very common species in the Antilles. Do you see the square shape of the tail? Look closely and you'll see a chestnut rump."

I laughed to myself. Could there ever have been a more James Bond *authenticus* reply? Even Fleming smiled and turned to me. "This wretched interview—what are your plans? Where are you staying? We must see more of you."

I told him and he said firmly, "You must stay for lunch. Take a swim while I go ahead with the interview, then we can talk."

I waved my hand towards Mrs. Fleming below us, snorkeling on a reef. "Mightn't she find unexpected guests inconvenient?"

"Not a bit of it," and he called down to two figures on beach chairs on the sand. "Come on up!" he shouted. "Mr. and Mrs. James Bond are here!" This time the name was spoken in capital letters. The figures were Mr. and Mrs. Hilary Bray, whom we learned later were long-time friends of the Flemings, and lovely people. She gave a start and again the scriptwriter was positively theatrical, for Mr. Bray held up in his hand the latest edition of *Birds of the West Indies* by James Bond, and we all broke out laughing. He was looking up the cave swallows!

The Brays took care of us. Fleming returned to his interview, and we had a superb swim in the small gem of a cove embraced by two headlands providing complete privacy. We met Mrs. Ian Fleming and I detected what I thought might be the case—not so warm a welcome. After Fleming sent the TV crew off to Oracabessa for lunch and we were all seated in a corner of the big room at the luncheon table, there was a strong undercurrent in our conversation of wondering what both Bond and Fleming were thinking. Had anything like this ever happened before? Conan Doyle's Sherlock Holmes is reported to have been a real doctor in Scotland, but they never met. And in those days there were no moving pictures to confuse the living doctor, the author, and Basil Rathbone's Sherlock Holmes. In the present case actor Sean Connery and Jim were much the same type, so it was no wonder that Alice in Wonderland conversations took place whenever Jim showed up.

Fleming wanted me to sit beside him, for he knew I would talk freely about Jim. I felt he was not entirely sure we hadn't something up our sleeves. At a certain turn in our conversation I mentioned that Jim had been to Harrow and Cambridge, and, like a shot came the query, "He's not an *English*-man?" I chuckled privately, recalling Jim's brief remark that Fleming would never have "stolen" a fellow countryman's name. Fine, I thought. Very satisfactory. I'm getting my pound of flesh in fine style.

"No," I replied. "But he did have a great-great-great uncle Phineas Bond who was the first British consul in Philadelphia after the revolution."

Fleming relaxed and I went on about Jim's early days in the Caribbean, living with the natives, and eating their food. Again Fleming spoke sharply, "How's he fixed for money now?

So the poor fellow *was* worried and I said soothingly, "He gets by," and we both glanced across the table at Jim. Presently he said seriously, "Anyone who's referred to your husband's books as often as I have knows he's been to more West Indian islands than probably anyone who has ever lived. You must write up his experiences, you know, for what's actually happened to him outshines anything I've made my James Bond do!"

"Scarcely that, and heaven forbid!" I exclaimed. He went on urging me to write—to put Jim's experiences on tape and turn them over to any TV producer. "They'd eat them up," he persisted.

After we'd had our coffee I said to Mrs. Fleming, "I feel sure everyone takes a siesta after lunch and we are leaving immediately."

"Wait a minute," Fleming said, and disappeared into another room to return with a guest book. He flipped it open and handed it to Jim who began to sign his name when he was stopped by Fleming's turning to another page. "You've got to have a page all to yourself, and write it *big*!" I also signed my name and he màde a big X over the whole page, and said, "Before you go I want to give you a copy of my new book. But it isn't out yet so you must not let anyone see it 'til it's on the market."

This time he was gone a little longer and came back with a copy of *You Only Live Twice*. On the fly page he had written "To the real James Bond, from the Thief of his identity, Ian Fleming, February 5, 1964—a Great Day!"

News of this encounter got around. Hero meets Author. Newspapers and magazines picked it up, the amusing confusion catching people's fancy. And then in August we were in Maine that foggy night when Walter Cronkite wound up his program saying "Coming up—requiem for a myth-maker—after this message."

Although we knew about his heart attacks, it was with a distinct shock that we now heard of Fleming's death. There had been a strong feeling of respect on both sides during those short hours together on that February day at Golden Eye. I sent photographs to the Brays and he replied, "It was a red-letter day to Ian and he used to reflect on it happily. When he got back to England he used to relate it as 'The Story of the Year, Golden Eye, 1964.'"

After this we thought the legend would die down, but we were wrong. Episodes kept recurring and we became tired of explaining how Fleming had "stolen" Jim's name. In Trinidad we had to call on the manager of a bank to cash Jim's check. Although he signed his name several times on a piece of paper to prove who he was, the teller bashfully said, "You could have practiced that, sir." On the Main Line a cinema theatre manager called up and told Jim he would give him $100.00 if he'd arrive by helicopter at his theatre on the opening night of *Goldfinger*. He declined.

I frequently thought of Fleming's advice to write up Jim's early experiences in the West Indies and, in a way, that is what I was already doing except that I was including my own travels with him. Then one day, after a board meeting of the Philadelphia Free Library of Philadelphia, I walked across Logan Square with Seymour Adelman, a fellow board member and chairman of the rare book committee, and received almost the same advice. Seymour, however, laid emphasis on the humorous episodes that were still happening to Jim and me. Sometime later, after having sent him a newspaper clipping for his collection of Churchilliana, he wrote:

"Your letter from Antigua on the tribulations of being the real James Bond is very amusing. I wonder whether you realize just how entertaining these adventures really are? What you must do now is to write up a full length article on this entrancing subject and send it off to *The New Yorker* or the *Atlantic Monthly* or *Harper's*. I predict that any one of them would jump at the chance to publish it. Mind now—this is not a suggestion but an *order* on the behalf of all James Bond fans."

I found it an awesome thing to be a member of Seymour's rare book committee. It was a world in itself, quite different from the monthly board meetings. It's a book collector's world—his specialty, the English literary world. He knew more about London than possibly anyone in our country, yet he had never been there, a statement he refused to accept. "Never been there?" he'd exclaim. "I spent all last winter in 17th and 18th century London!" As a collector of rare books himself, his long-range view of what was important in the past, and might be in the future, impressed me. It was also interesting to compare his advice with Fleming's. Fleming aimed at TV, Hollywood and dollars for himself, while Seymour aimed at rare books to enhance not only the library's collection but his own.

So one day I took out everything in my files, got a good many chuckles out of them, and in a light-hearted fashion put them all together, cast about for a title and came up with HOW 007 GOT HIS NAME. It was too long for an article and too short for a book but I sent it off to Mr. Collins in London, knowing that he at least knew who James Bond was. What I didn't know at the time was that "bird" to an Englishman is synonymous with what we call a pretty girl—a "chick" or a "quail." The fact that James Bond was a curator of birds tickled Mr. Collins's sense of humor and gave me the pleasure of writing to Seymour from Maine that the Collins Publishers of London wished to publish the manuscript in the form of a book.

Seymour instantly replied: "I am delighted! And I am more inclined to congratulate Collins than you, for that perceptive publishing house now has on its list an item that Bondiana collectors will prize today and a hundred years from now!"

After the book was on the stands in London, selling for ten shillings and sixpence (about $2.50 at that time), Mr. Collins asked me which American publisher I would like to have. Think of that! I was in a position to choose my publisher! I named three but Mr. Collins was unsuccessful. About fourteen American publishers would have nothing to do with it. The book was too small, too short. I never found out the whole story but suspect the deal offered by Collins and Co. favored themselves more than any U.S. publisher. Also, the American public never took to the 007 books with the British enthusiasm, preferring the Hollywood version of Fleming's early books. It is too bad more people here did not read them, for Fleming's early books have a certain magic charm that the movies lack.

Every book has its own career, zero up to "two million sold before publication," and, as I look back, these sixty-two little pages had a "jolly good time." They appeared inside a fetching dust jacket combining exotic bird feathers and an automatic hand gun by the same artist who had designed many of Fleming's 007 books. The story made a bright flash in France, Belgium, Italy, Sweden and Great Britain, and recently in West Germany. The French brought out a mini-paperback called *Comment 007 Chipa Son Nom*, and the result of all this was the very opposite of what I'd expected. Instead of ending the matter as far as Jim and I were concerned, it stirred up a whirlwind of publicity. Even in Chestnut Hill, on Germantown Avenue, my old friend Marion Rivinus stopped me one morning and said, "Hi, there! I hear you've gone international on us!" "Oh yes," I replied. "I'm only trying to keep up with you—*you* famous Distinguished Woman of Pennsylvania!"

But Seymour was on the right track. About ten years after publication the book appeared in a collector's catalogue priced at $5.00. A few years later he sent me another catalogue encircling the book now valued at

141

$35.00, and in the 1980's at an auction held at an American Ornithological Union Conference, Kansas City, it sold for $75.00.

The jolliest time of all was the summer it came out. This was the same summer when two international bird conferences in England were to draw together distinguished ornithologists from all over the globe. After the annual meeting of the International Council for Bird Preservation, which was to meet at Cambridge University, Jim was to read a paper entitled "Affinities of the Antillean Avifauna" at the International Ornithological Congress at Oxford. Also very much on his mind was the fifth edition of his *Birds of the West Indies* which was being produced by Collins and Co. This would mean many consultations in the publishers' offices just around the corner from the Stafford Hotel where we were staying.

Upon our arrival at the hotel the little blonde receptionist, apparently familiar with the Sean Connery version of 007, looked up at Jim and murmured "Amyzing!" What was amazing to me was the welcome received in the small reception room off the lobby. Mr. Burdet, the hotel manager, was there, and there were flowers from him as well as from the publishers. Also reporters and photographers. *The Evening Standard* was already running a banner headline, "Mr. and Mrs. James Bond Arrive in London!" Upstairs in our room I found a memorandum for scheduled interviews "laid on" by the Collins people. But there was also a cheerful note from Adrian House, the editor who was taking care of my little book, saying they had just sold the serial rights to *Le Soir* the Brussels evening paper which was netting us a tidy little sum. Everyone was happy! And I was even happier when I found among my mail a clipping from Seymour picturing a cocktail shaker, two stemmed glasses and a gun lying carelessly between them with the caption "Have a vodka martini (stirred—not shaken) in the new 007 Room at the London Hilton." In Seymour's handwriting at the bottom, "Obviously your first stop in London!"

Fun and fame! I felt like a movie star but was definitely concerned. Over our whiskey sours that evening I admitted as much to Jim. The situation would have to be handled carefully, for Jim was definitely not in the mood to play the part of 007.

"It's your book so you've got to take care of the whole thing," he said. I replied, "The trouble is *you* are the person the reporters are after." "Well, a bit of both perhaps. But I'm counting on you to leave me out of it. All of it. And," he added, "don't tell me you won't enjoy every minute of it."

He was right. I had been thinking of all the people scattered all over

142

the countryside who were making money out of 007. So why shouldn't I get at least as much fun as possible out of the scenario? But how to do it while ignoring the key figure? I was especially uneasy about the scheduled interviews. I hadn't the vaguest idea of what English reporters were like face-to-face. My reactions are too quick and inclined to be frivolous and I could easily be trapped into saying something idiotic.

In the classical tradition of polite relationships between publisher and author, I was invited out to lunch by Adrian House. He took me to Pruniers just around the corner, and as we swung into step together it occurred to me that of course Adrian was just the right person to brief me on how to behave with the hometown press.

"Say the book was just something you had to get out of your system. You know, you just dashed it off. Did it for a lark," he advised.

Rather drily I said, "Fleming referred to that bird when he spoke of writing his *Casino Royale*. He said that he knew something about gambling and the Secret Service and thought it would be jolly to combine the two. It was a lark to write."

Adrian nodded his fair young head and I got the impression that, generally speaking, a light-hearted book, if not exactly unimportant, was after all of little consequence.

I need not have worried about the interviews. The London reporters' respect for Jim's desire for privacy was refreshing. In fact, his public image as a man of mystery only enhanced their fun on playing up the "oh, so secret angles." At Cambridge, however, an enterprising reporter for the *Cambridge News* fell so deeply under the influence of the secret agent routine that on the day of the International Council of Bird Preservation meeting he managed (confessing so later) to cover all entries to Cambridge from London—motor car, helicopter or train. But we fell into his trap at the Cambridge railroad depot. Jim's mind was wrapped up in his speech as well as in his memories of his former years at Trinity College, his shooting companions and his bicycling back and forth from Cambridge to his home in Buckinghamshire where he had lived with his father and stepmother.

It was a bit of a shock to see facing us in the middle of the waiting room a large blackboard chalked up with the following: "Message for James Bond—Please call at the Enquiry Office."

This meant the ticket office we supposed, and when Jim presented himself, a piece of paper was handed to him bearing a telephone number. Feeling it might be something from the Bird Preservation Council, he made the call and was bewildered when it turned out that the person at the other end merely wished to know if he'd gotten the message. He

143

said yes, and the trap snapped shut. A youth with a camera and a pretty girl pounced on him from behind. Outwitted, Jim could do little else but laugh, and permitted himself to be photographed outside the University Arms. He then escaped to the Blue Boar for lunch with his half-brother Tristram Eeles and I was captured by Cedric Tennant, the photographer, and Olive Nelson, the reporter.

They took me to lunch at a small restaurant and we had a splendid talk about the newspaper business—especially small town papers like theirs and my *Chestnut Hill Local*. The next morning Olive's story in *The Cambridge Times* was headed "Pussy Galore Leads 007 a Dog's Life." There were two horrendous photographs of me, one smiling, "Sometimes it's fun," the other grimacing, "but not at three A.M.." Adrian told me later they couldn't keep up with requests for it.

Back in London on a rainy day, I met Fleming's secretary, "Griffie," who had invited me for lunch. I was to meet her at her office at Bucklersbury House where Glidrose Publications had their offices. Beryl Griffie Williams was exactly what I had expected from her letters— fiftyish, big boned, white-haired, efficient, independent and knowledge-able. Her office was lined with bookcases of Fleming's first editions in a dozen languages, three-foot square scrap books, photographs and cartoons. Since Fleming's death she had lost heart in it and hated the big business, money-power racket which was all that now survived. The glamour and the fun were over now that Fleming was no longer around.

I saw a good deal of Griffie. She took me to lunch that day through a weird back alley-way to Banksend Street and The Anchor Café, Ben Johnson's Tavern-on-the-Thames. Seymour Adelman would have been beside himself with joy if he'd been with us. The tiny brick house huddled close to the river bank and inside the aroma of the past was overwhelming. The panelled walls were hung with coats of arms, and a portrait of Ben Johnson's prodigious mistress hung over an antiquated carved mantel.

Griffie said the lamb chops were especially good here, and to go with them we ordered a bottle of Graves. Naturally our conversation centered around Fleming and her many years as his secretary. She told me some extraordinary things which are not right for me to publicize and I said, "You are certainly sitting on a gold mine, aren't you? What a story you could tell!"

"Right you are, but I shall never tell it. I'm pretty sure one day I'll leave England, for Australia perhaps, or New Zealand, where I have friends."

For several years we kept in touch with each other but now, in the

1980s, I have lost track of her. She was a lovely, understanding sort of person and I was glad to have met her.

I knew of course, despite what she told me, that Fleming had been a controversial figure and that already a variety of books were appearing about him: Kingsley Amis's *The James Bond Dossier*, with the sub-title "Is He in Hell or is He in Heaven, That Dammed Illusive 007?;" Henry Zeigler's *Ian Fleming: The Spy Who Came in with the Gold*; Ann Boyd's *The Devil With James Bond*; and Lieutenant Colonel Bill Thompson's *The Book of James Bond* or *Every Man His Own 007*. There were others exploiting every imaginable angle, offensive, cheap, flippant, and at times downright libelous.

It was John Pearson who gave us a thorough, sensitive picture of Fleming in his *Alias James Bond—the Life of Ian Fleming*, published by McGraw Hill two years after Fleming's death. The very title of this book indicates the unique relationship between Fleming and his fictional character. John pearson makes a point of showing us how the fictional James Bond became a reality not only to Fleming but to his friends as well. No one referred to him except occasionally as 007. And after each of his thirteen 007 books was completed Fleming admitted, "It was a jerk to come back to reality." My reading of Pearson's inside-out biography had a similar effect on me, and I am only too thankful that the James Bond I look at every day is a flesh and blood reality.

CHAPTER 11

1972–1977

ONE DOES NOT have to be married to a naturalist to know that if any living creature fails to adapt itself to its environment it dies. As I moved into my seventies it was hard to distinguish whether I was degenerating physically or if my environment was skidding off the tracks. The whole world seemed to be writhing in a whirl of constant violence. Demonstrations against the Vietnam War I could understand, but why the assassinations of President Kennedy, Martin Luther King, and Robert Kennedy? Catastrophic explosions of violence were taking place everywhere, except in small areas like Chestnut Hill. True, even we did not escape flurries of burglaries, desperate local addicts stealing radios and TV sets, quick dollars to be exchanged for cocaine and other drugs.

But my six step-grandchildren, like many others around them, despite their belonging to World War II's "baby boom" generation, have not become hippies, flower children, drug addicts or drop-outs in society. Quite the reverse. They are growing up to prove themselves intelligent and public-spirited. Despite the double generation gap between us and the strain of very different lifestyles, they hold the future of the country in their hands and I intend to find what I can in them to respect and applaud. I am finding plenty right here in my own community—serious-minded and courageous young people with a strong sense of mission and the fibre to face the tremendous challenges ahead. I also sympathize with them and have a personal feeling of indebtedness to them for keeping me from becoming a pessimistic, censorious old woman fuss-cat.

At times, however, it is difficult not to be pessimistic. In 1973, Frank Rizzo cast covetous eyes on my old stamping-ground, City Hall, and ran for mayor. This brought Joe Clark into action again. It was "crystal clear" that Joe did not want Rizzo to become mayor, and he said, "Dick Dilworth, Jim Tate and I were all active in the National League of Cities but Rizzo has been to none of their meetings. He debauched the police department and the civil service by using federal funds to hire his stooges and has polarized the city, black versus white, rich versus poor. Everything will go to hell if he gets another four years."

Rizzo won nevertheless, elected as a Democrat but supporting Nixon's presidency. He also tried to get the charter changed so that he could run for a third term, but in this he failed.

Joe has always been sincerely concerned about good government, and for years has been a strong supporter of the World Court. It's a pity we lost him as a senator, but I feel that his scholarly and enlightened remarks far outnumber his political diatribes. And I agreed heartily when he said, "In many ways the 1972 election was a test of character of the American people, and they flunked. I see a serious decline in our national fibre—idealism, unselfishness, standards of decency and efforts to reform national unity."

He regarded himself as obsolete and believed his influence in Philadelphia affairs was nominal. But there are more than a few of us who still recall the courageous and exciting days of the Clark and Dilworth period. We will never forget the day Joe walked on stage at the Academy of Music to deliver his inaugural address, prompting Nathaniel Burt to say that "Joe Clark was the most effective reformer in Philadelphia history."

Joe's frequent comments about decency and idealism came back to me again and again as the Watergate scandal and the near impeachment of Richard Nixon engulfed and horrified the nation. Although astronaut Neil Armstrong had exclaimed "One small step for man, one giant leap for mankind" when he stepped on the moon, I could not help feeling that humans back on earth were degenerating at a sickening pace. For the next few years social disorder and political conspiracy broke all records. One kept on hoping that those in high government would begin to help us feel confident in their leadership. But when the Watergate scandal began to unfold we could not believe it was happening in the middle of the twentieth century. We thought we were civilized. Now sabotage, espionage and conspiracy were exposed day by day. People met each other in elevators, trains and trolleys and on the streets, stopping to share the disgraceful news in the daily headlines and over the television. You'd catch the eye of a friend in the market, forget your food list and rush together to moan over the awful picture of our government in disarray. Then came the televised Senate hearings chaired by Senator Sam J. Ervin of North Carolina.

It was impossible not to be impressed by him—a white-haired old southern gentleman who liked to describe himself as "a little old back-country lawyer." When he opened the proceedings saying, "Oh, what a tangled web we weave, when first we practice to deceive!" he became the first public figure of note who gave the rest of us some hope that maybe justice would be done. I scarcely missed a meeting of those televised proceedings, noting every mannerism, every remark made by the committee members, as well as by those who were brought in to answer questions. The whole performance was theatrical, dreadful, exciting and revealing. All of us on the sidelines, in front of our television screens, could only keep on hoping that something drastic would be done to clean up the mess.

Nor were we disappointed. Presidential advisers, cabinet members and White House aides were dismissed, and Richard Nixon was compelled by the Supreme Court and public pressure to release the secret tapes he had made in the White House. When these were made public, I think that just about everyone was ashamed of the vulgar talk, crude language and vicious glee with which the conspirators concocted plans to outwit their "enemies."

In the midst of this performance Vice-President Agnew resigned, having been accused of receiving bribes and kick-backs in unmarked envelopes. Nixon nominated Gerald Ford as Vice-President, who modestly warned us, "I am a Ford, not a Lincoln." Then in May 1974, the House Judiciary Committee began formal hearings on the impeachment of Richard Nixon. In August Nixon resigned as president, and in September President Ford granted him a "full, free and absolute pardon for any crimes he may have committed."

To my father there was always a blot on the Stars and Stripes. He believed slavery in the south could have been ended without bloodshed. Richard Nixon had had great potential, his successful trip to China in 1972 just one proof of this. But to me the sad story of his abuse of presidential power is a similar blot on the flag.

If the 1970's was a depressing time politically it was also a shattering phase in our personal lives even though the decade started off propitiously. Collins of London and Houghton Mifflin of Boston brought out a second revised edition of Jim's *Birds of the West Indies*; my book *Far Afield in the Caribbean* was also on the stands. Our social life flowed along normally with pleasant dinner-parties—delightful occasions especially for the ladies who never get tired of showing off their new evening dresses. I basked in the fleeting glory of headlines in the local newspapers, autographing parties and, best of all, letters from friends and strangers who take the trouble not only to read what you write but to write and tell you so.

Two of our friends, Charlie and Ruth Patrick Hodge, went so far as to give a huge party in honor of our books at their Chestnut Hill house, "Viburnam Ridge." Invitation styles had changed and we were no longer restricted to old-fashioned formal engraving. The Hodges sent out an attractive green edged card with green lettering featuring two green iguanas chasing each other's tails on the upper left hand corner. This was but one of the many delightful illustrations from my book, drawn by Elizabeth R. Leyden, daughter of my friend Marion Rivinus. Ruth Seltzer was among the guests at the Hodge's party and reported in her *Sunday Inquirer* column that Brandon Barringer had told her he had "gulped the book," and that Sturgis Ingersoll had read it with an open Atlas beside him because he'd "never heard of some of the islands."

It was shortly after my marriage to Jim that I met Ruth Hodge. One day she invited me to lunch at the Acorn Club. I knew that she and Jim had known each other for many years at the Academy of Natural Sciences where she was known as Dr. Patrick, curator of the Limnology Department and a specialist in diatoms. I had heard of her remarkable career and was quite startled when she said, "I have a job for you as a writer. I want you to write about rivers and do for rivers what Rachel Carson did for air pollution in her *Silent Spring.*" I could only smile and confess that I wouldn't even know where to begin. But that luncheon was the beginning of a long and close friendship.

Indeed, Ruth Patrick Hodge stands alone in what she has accomplished in the control of water pollution. Time and time again she has brought environmentalists and offending industrialists together by simply asking, "Why not reach an agreement to get scientific facts, then spend the necessary money to improve the river, rather than spend money on delays and lawyers' fees when you have a confrontation?" She worked for the old Atomic Energy Commission, for DuPont, and for the Department of Energy, and has made surveys of many of the nation's rivers. Throughout the years her amazing collection of awards is a subject she refuses to talk about or allow others to describe. Like all true scientists she lives through her work. Yet she manages to allow time for friendships and hospitality, and enjoys bringing congenial people together.

This ongoing friendship with Ruth Hodge also recalled my youthful ambition to find true companionship. My success in doing so under many happy circumstances has taught me that there are as many kinds of friendships as there are people. Each relationship is different from any other, and fortunately the world is large enough to make room for them all. I dwell on this subject because in one's seventies so many friends disappear, and those who remain become increasingly important. I was thus deeply depressed when my sister died in 1973. I had now outlived all of my immediate family. Jim was in the same situation and we shared a kind of strange new loneliness, fraught with the inescapable awareness that our own capacities for "living it up" were declining. Travel, for example, an essential part of Jim's life, was becoming difficult for us both. Our trips to the West Indies had lost much of their glamour, although Jim always managed to pick up new data for his work, and we kept in touch with our friends down there. Maurice and Hazel Hutt in Barbados usually had interesting news; the Patrick Tenisons at Good Hope Plantation in Jamaica never failed to make room for us, and we made a point whenever possible of visiting George and Hazel Eggleston in St. Lucia.

Meanwhile, my outlook on life was far from cheerful. I began to worry about my health. Our friend Dr. Joe Hollander, who knows everything about bursitis, arthritis, and aching joints told us to beware of "thinking old." He advised, "Just say to yourself, 'I don't feel thirty-five as often as I used to.'" But I made the rounds of doctors, X-rays, blood tests and examinations. Every doctor told me there was nothing wrong, just a little high blood pressure perhaps. "Take your pills," they said, "and go out and enjoy life."

But there was something wrong. I was permitting myself to become irritated by a host of trivial things. I was dwelling on everything that was sad. I was building up a fear of old age and inescapable infirmities, allowing myself to rebel constantly against bodily discomforts. I cringed over the personal disasters that had befallen so many of my friends. I bemoaned my inability to play the piano as well as I used to. I convinced myself I could never summon up enough energy to write another book, that I was now reduced to a sonnet here and there, or pleasant little articles for magazines and newspapers kind enough to print them.

In such a frame of mind I came home from the West Indies in March 1974 not knowing it would be our last trip there. In May we gave a large party at 721 Davidson Road when the pink dogwoods were at their best and the wood thrushes were singing. Again, we were blissfully unaware that this would be our last entertainment on a large scale. We spent July and August in Maine as usual; winced in September over Ford's pardon to Nixon; entertained Joe and Iris Clark; and in December faced a cancer operation for Jim at the Chestnut Hill Hospital. This changed our entire pattern of life—physical, social and spiritual.

The shock of what we were up against dispelled my dreary attitude overnight. Here was something *really* to be concerned about. It was as if a mountain had suddenly been set before us, a mountain that we had to climb together with a steadfast belief that something important for us both lay beyond. We *had* to climb that mountain. Doctors, nurses, new knowledge in surgery and radiology, and especially friends and family, were the ropes that helped us over the worst places and kept us on the trail.

It was to be a long, long trail with highlights as well as moments of despair. It is amazing as I look back that, despite our inability to go south for the next three years, we managed to get to Maine. The magnetic appeal and the healing atmosphere of our quiet cove became as important as any treatments that doctors or medical science could offer. Even packing up for camp, however tedious, was a cheerful task. Finally the moment comes when we tuck the last articles in the Buick's trunk: typewriter, waffle-iron, overnight bags and a picnic lunch, then say goodbye to Margaret McClintock, a familiar scene for both of us for many years. Even the step-grandchildren agreed with Margaret that we always "came back from Maine in better shape than when we went up." We also looked forward to the end of the journey, knowing that down at the bottom of our road through spruce and pine and cedar, Verna and John Hodgdon would be there to greet us. Verna and I always rushed into each others' arms with a big hug, her eyes always filling with tears at either end of our stay. Margaret and Verna—two special friends, who for almost half a century have strewn my path with roses and comforted me in times of trouble.

During this summer of 1975 we all hoped Maine's magic would hasten Jim's convalescence, for in September the Academy of Natural Sciences was bestowing the coveted Leidy Medal on him at a symposium on zoögeography in the Caribbean. This award was established in 1925 to celebrate the hundredth anniversary of Joseph Leidy (1825–1891), a nineteenth-century naturalist, professor of natural history at Swarthmore College, Chairman of the Biology Department at the University of Pennsylvania and Chairman of the Board of Curators at the Philadelphia Academy of Sciences. The award is one of the most prestigious for basic research in the natural sciences and is awarded about every three years for the "best publication, exploration, discovery or research in the natural sciences." Distinguished professors and naturalists from a dozen universities and institutions are on the list of its recipients.

Frank Gill, director of the symposium and curator of birds at the Academy, sent Jim a letter while we were in Maine describing the symposium program. It was to begin at 9:00 A.M. in the auditorium of the Free Library across Logan Square from the Academy. The list of people expected to attend (which Frank also sent us) covered natural history museums across the nation, as well as including some from abroad.

Coffee and a lunch break would be held at the Academy, and at 5 P.M. the Leidy Award ceremony would take place back at the library. Jim felt he could manage the informal luncheon and the presentation but certainly not the reception and dinner. It was very much on his mind that after all these elaborate proceedings he must make a supreme effort to appear for the award.

September nineteenth arrived, and of course it was Ruth Hodge who had gotten ahead of me and arranged for a limousine and chauffeur to drive us from 721 Davidson Road into the Academy for the luncheon. Afterwards we were driven around Logan Square to the library and found that people were still pouring into the auditorium. Among them was the figure of a very tall black woman moving majestically down an aisle looking for a seat. She was dressed in what was obviously native West Indian style. Folds of pink and white peppermint-striped silk fell loosely from one shoulder over a voluptuous satin dress of peacock blue. Her head was wrapped in a kind of turban of blue and silver cloth, and enormous circles of gold dangled from her ears. She stood out in that assembly of proper Philadelphians like a personage from another world, daring, regal, historically romantic. Naturally we all talked about her later, wondering if perhaps she had read in the newspapers that a "Caribbean Symposium" was to be held on a certain date at the Free Library of Philadelphia, and had expected some sort of West Indian carnival. What were her thoughts when the professors on the stage did nothing but talk about birds, fossils, butterflies and bats? I was sorry she did not stay so I could speak to her, but understood when she got up pretty soon and left the auditorium.

The only offbeat incident occurred when I decided I needed a breath of fresh air. I was tired and anxious about Jim and, leaving my aisle seat on the front row, I slipped through a door at the end of the aisle and found myself in a small vestibule. Then I opened the street door and set off the fire alarm! What a terrible noise! One of the Library guards came to the rescue, switched off the alarm, gave me a grin, and I returned to my seat in disgrace.

When it came time for Jim to go to the platform I could see he was more dazed than nervous. He apologized for having to read his paper sitting down but got through it very well. Ruth Hodge introduced him with a few words and read a letter from Ernst Mayr, Director of the Museum of Comparative Zoölogy at Harvard. He had written that the Leidy award was especially dear to him as it had been his first honor when he was "young and struggling." He emphasized his congratulations to Jim, adding that "all the recent activity on the birds of the West Indies would be impossible but for the foundation you laid."

When Ruth presented the medal, Jim looked as if he scarcely knew where he was and I was anxious to get him to the front door of the library and into the limousine waiting to drive him home. I watched the car drive off with him sitting alone in the back seat, pulled myself together and prepared myself for the dinner and reception. Everything went off smoothly. There were further tributes to Jim, and it was amusing to look for your seating card, as the tables were not numbered but identified by birds, and I found myself among "Copper-rumped hummingbirds!" Other tables bore such names as "Chestnut-bellied Chlorophonia," and "Blue-headed Quail Doves." Someone also had the original idea of providing an *obbligato* to the proceedings by playing a cassette of bird songs. With the tropical bird noises—guffaws, shrieks, squawks, screams and the nerve-wracking crescendo of the ant-wren—conversation was impossible. After it was all over Charlie and Ruth drove me home and I could not help thinking that St. Luke had stumbled a little when he'd said, "A prophet is not without honor save in his own country."

It was taking time to realize what had truly happened to us. The highlights were deeply gratifying, but nothing takes the place of good health. We were grounded. No more *Queen Elizabeths* to Southampton or the dear little *S.S. Flandre*, or the *Gripsholm*. No more crossing the channel from Dover to Calais, then taking *La Flèche d'Or* to Paris. All the delicious little touches enjoyed in continental travel now belonged to our past, such as putting shoes outside your bedroom door and discovering them in the morning bright and shining. No more coming back to your hotel after dinner and finding that the *femme de chambre* has placed *Monsieur's* pajamas on his bed, his slippers on the floor, and has folded *Madam's* pale blue nightgown neatly on her bed. Even the waste baskets would have been emptied, ash trays cleaned, and fresh towels placed in the bathroom. Bedside lights would also be turned on, the shutters closed and the window curtains drawn. Never again would there be our little rhyme over the telephone in the morning to room service for "*Deux complets, s'il vous plait, un café, un de thé.*"

How glad we were to have travelled so much! How thankful to have programmed our invisible computers with so many wonderful places and people, who at the tap of a button, figuratively speaking, could now present themselves before our eyes. Obviously my new rôle was not to fling myself into politics, matriarchy, or social *grande damery*. We might be grounded but only on the surface, and all at once the dozens of notebooks I had filled and diaries I had kept during the past seventy-odd years became important. As long as my eyesight and mental stability held out, I could always write.

And there was always something to write about. I had often thought of skimming the cream from *Far Afield in the Caribbean* and *How 007 Got His Name*, refresh the mixture with up-to-date travels, wrap it all together in one book and call it *To James Bond With Love*. Why not? My whole attention was concentrated on Jim at the time, and the moment I started out on the project the mere falling into the routine of another book cheered me up immensely.

Another summer at Pretty Marsh helped to put both of us on our feet again. And once back home on Davidson Road we made a drastic change in our daily routine. We decided to have the big meal of the day at lunch time, with supper a simple repast that was easy to put together. This meant that Margaret McClintock would come to the house directly after breakfast, instead of after lunch, perform the daily household duties and cook "dinner" for us at twelve-thirty. It all worked out very well; Margaret was particularly pleased to drive home now in daylight instead of in the dark, especially during the wintertime.

We were also beginning to think that Oscar Stonorov's "cottage" at 721 Davidson Road was becoming a little too much for us. Nathaniel Hawthorne's title *House of Seven Gables* suggested that 721 be called *House of Seven Stairways*. There were two flights of eight steps each from the street down to the front door; two stairways hanging on the mahogany beam that cut the house through the middle, two flights on the terraces west of the house, and, on the east side, a treacherous rocky, raggedy-ann down-hill path through holly and rhododendron bushes. As both bedrooms were on the ground floor, a convalescent had to tackle either one stairway inside, or two outside, to reach the automobile. My knees were also beginning to object to all the stairways, but there was no particular hurry about selling the place. However, we did put our name down for an apartment in the Hill House on West Evergreen Avenue, and went about our daily schedules.

December always seemed to have a grudge against us, and this year we ran into double trouble. Jim was stricken with septicaemia and rushed by ambulance to Jefferson Hospital in town, and Shippen's youngest daughter, Louise Lewis Page was killed in an automobile accident in

155

Maine. She was known in Philadelphia for the leading role she had played in rounding up a group of women's charitable organizations and incorporating them in what is now known as "Women's Way." A memorial service was held for her at St. Paul's Church, which was full to overflowing as it had been for her father. A friend, Marjorie Bacon, wrote a poem for the occasion, and the last lines sent a shock through the congregation because her voice sounded so much like Louise's: "'Don't mourn for me!' I hear your clear voice say, 'Get on with it! I'm with you all the way!'"

CHAPTER 12

1977–1986

WE KNEW THE TIME had come to sell the house and put ourselves with confidence and hope into the hands of David Eichler, who insists that a house usually "Finds its own owner." Just how this happens is difficult to describe, but 721 Davidson apparently knew what it wanted and got it when it "found" E. Crosby Willett, Chestnut Hill's stained glass window artist. He and his wife Gussie knew precisely how to handle the place and moved in on the heels of our departure just before Christmas in 1977.

Then the Willetts gave a housewarming which I wouldn't have missed for anything. It was stupendous! All the patio lights were turned on, showing the terraces outside and the deepening woods beyond. Inside there was nothing but candlelight and a huge fire burning on the seven-foot wide hearth. The twenty-foot high living room was in its element. Upstairs in the dining room every sort of Christmas cheer was at hand and you could pause at the big mahogany railing and toast everyone below as well as those at eye level. How delighted Oscar Stonorov would have been to see it.

As for us, fate played one of its sly tricks on me. Twenty years ago, along with Lloyd Wells and most everyone else in Chestnut Hill, I had cried "What? A high-rise apartment house in Chestnut Hill? Never!" But here I was moving into it and glad to do so. As the manager was showing me around and I exclaimed with joy over the deluge of sunlight pouring through the twenty-two foot bay window, he replied drily, "Wait until it's summer time and the air conditioning goes off."

Our friends like to tease us about our "penthouse" (there are seven other eleventh floor apartments in Hill House similar to ours), and Helen and Walter West, experts at teasing, sent us a huge bouquet of flowers the day we moved in with the message in Helen's handwriting, "Congratulations! You've made it to the Top o' the Hill at last!"

157

During the first three years of our marriage I had had a taste of apartment living and had secretly sworn never to live in an apartment again. But things were very different now. Life at Hill House in my familiar Chestnut Hill was quite different from life in town at the Drake Hotel. I expected to feel restricted and at times did have spells of claustrophobia. But I had not forgotten that you had to adapt yourself to your environment or shrivel up and blow away. As for Jim, I had no fears. Although he had lived in his father's two extensive estates, one in Gwynedd Valley and the other in England, he was also well acquainted with boarding-house rooms, inns, hotels, bungalows, tropical shelters, native huts and finally the Crillon Hotel on Rittenhouse Square, Philadelphia. His one fear was that I'd expect him to become a member of the "Chestnut Hill cocktail set." I comforted him by saying there wasn't such a thing and that I didn't belong to anything like it. He sighed with relief, adding, "At least Chestnut Hill is half an hour closer to Maine."

This was the fifth neighborhood in the community where I was to consider myself at home. Marion Rivinus, downstairs in her second floor apartment, told me, "Of course an apartment is never really like home." But I was vastly relieved with the simplification of our domestic life and found the view from our eleventh floor windows extraordinarily home-like. The largest trees facing the city are giant oaks, sycamores and beech trees, some of their branches high enough to break the wide horizon. Looking downward I can stretch out my arms and embrace my whole life spread out below—a ninety year span of intimacy and love for this particular corner of Philadelphia. Bounded on the west and south by the Wissahickon and Cresheim Creeks, and on the north by Stenton and Northwestern Avenues, everything I have learned, experienced and dreamed about has sprung from this "down home" habitat.

A dozen miles to the south beyond the invisible Delaware River the pale blue line of New Jersey evokes the Atlantic Ocean, while the City of Brotherly Love rides at anchor on the horizon like a monstrous aircraft carrier. At times the afterglow from the setting sun can turn the towers and buildings of Philadelphia into a dream city of glowing pure white marble. At just such an hour Bud Gilchrist, inheriting some of his father's artistic powers, used his telescopic lens to photograph this magnificent view. I had two of the enlarged prints framed, one for ourselves, the other for the Hill House offices.

On clear days through binoculars we can identify the towers of the Walt Whitman Bridge across the Delaware to Camden, the Benjamin Franklin Bridge, the Tacony-Palmyra, and the bridge from Pennsylvania to the New Jersey Turnpike. One afternoon through the bird-glasses I watched a freighter sail under the Tacony-Palmyra bridge and felt that indeed I was not cooped up in a stuffy old apartment but romantically in touch with far away ocean lanes and foreign cities. At night, the wide-flung curve is a belt of glowing emeralds, rubies and glittering diamonds. Early in the morning, looking toward the south, you can often see a scarf of rising mist floating in the lush greenery which indicates the course of the Cresheim Creek. Glance to the west and there will be two similar strands of silvery vapor revealing the whereabouts of the Wissa-hickon and the Schuylkill river. Even a rainy day can be beautiful. The sea of gently moving masses of different shades of green does not hide familiar roof-tops or the four-spired church tower of St. Martin-in-the-Fields.

Soon I was comfortably settled in my new writing room surrounded by the familiar writing desk, typewriter, book-shelves and steel files, and began to write again, or rather take up where I had left off after leaving Davidson Road. I no longer worked at the Cresheim Valley studio, having turned it over to Phoebe Valentine and her husband, the new owners of the Woodward property on which it stands.

My new book *To James Bond With Love* was in its final stages and was published in the fall of 1980 by Sutter House. To everyone's astonishment it appeared in *The Inquirer's* best seller list. But after the usual attention paid to it, interviews, and Sessler's autographing party, I found myself deflated. I had experienced that same sensation long ago in the 1920s. After slaving over a sonnet I made the appalling discovery that I was drained and had nothing else to say. Dismayed, I began writing frantically and was rebuked by Hervey Allen who was then living in Charleston. "Don't write about trivial things," he said. "Let your experiences and emotions build up again until you have something important to say." I took his advice, but now in my eighties was it possible that I was simply burnt out? Then I remembered an old piece of biblical advice: "Cast thy bread upon the waters for thou shalt find it after many days."

"Bread" in 1980s vernacular meant money. But what did I have to offer of any value? The literary world I had known disappeared after World War II. *The Saturday Review of Literature* created by almost forgotten members of the Algonquin Round Table had fallen into different hands during what I privately was calling The Splintered Era. Somerset Maugham's formula for a proper literary composition, "a beginning, a middle, and an end," was obsolete. The world of fiction which now attracted the greatest attention seemed to me lacking in beauty, rhythm or harmony. As for poetry, just write any sort of a sentence, break it up, slap the words into uneven lines and presto! Here is a poem! Television thrives on this splintered disorder. At one phase in the motion picture industry the camera was ordered to change its focal point every eight seconds. Television has cut this down to split seconds. I like Russell Baker's description of today's TV commercial news: " . . . a network of programs with a report of events without context, interrupted by scenes of blissfully recovered constipation followed by talking of the death of the human race followed by a smile."

What had all this to do with me? The sudden speculation occurred to me that I might have something to offer after all. The only way to find out its value was to give some of it away. So I collected my best poems, had them printed in a small pamphlet by the *Bar Harbor Times Press*, then made a prodigious list of all the persons still living with whom I shared a feeling of companionship. I called the booklet *White Swallow and Other Poems*, after a poem I had once written to Jim. Making out the list was exciting. I started with people I knew outside the U.S.A., then turned to those within the country, then Pennsylvania, Philadelphia, and finally Chestnut Hill. In each copy I wrote something personal and sent them off into the winds of chance like homing pigeons.

The result was overwhelming. It was one of the most rewarding experiences of my life. I was surprised that so many people read poetry and loved it. I even flushed out a number who wrote poetry themselves. It is clear that a poem is a private thing. People never exclaim, as they might over a novel, "By the way, I ran into a marvelous poem today!" Perhaps I felt something of the way E.B. White must have felt when he published his *My World and Welcome to It*.

Meanwhile our own private world was improving. Convalescence, even if slow, implies a return to good health and it cheered Jim a lot when he received still another award, this time a medal from the *Congreso Iberoamerica de Ornitologia* at their meeting held in Veracruz in Mexico. But we knew that neither of us could pick up the pace of our earlier days. We must now face "growing old gracefully." I actually know people who have done this, and Huberta Potter Sheaffer, former wife of Pennsylvania Governor George Earle, is one of them. Her motto is "old age is not for sissies."

Indeed it is a daily battle which starts the moment you awaken in the morning. You gather your wits together and slowly become aware that you are a conscious animal. But there is no leaping out of bed and jumping into today's schedule with a song in your heart. You lie still, feeling out the stiffness here and there, yawning, blinking your eyes and waiting for the will power to attack your morning exercises. Then you slip into the familiar routine of deep breathing, bicycling your legs, flopping around with the usual grunts when a knee, hip or shoulder joint protests. The next step is to sit on the edge of your bed, wonder if the philosophers of old went through this sort of thing, then stand up and teeter to the bathroom. The awful face in the mirror, the tousled hair, the blurred vision peering out at you makes you wonder who it is, teasing you cruelly with memories of sixty or fifty years ago when your skin was like rose petals and your luxuriant hair a mass of golden sunlight! Next comes the ordeal that civilization imposes upon you: getting into your clothes. This includes dropping a garment on the floor, the cry of anguish when you lean over and try to reach it, and, even worse, when you have to lean down and stay down to tie your arch-supporting shoes. Perhaps the hardest of all, until you've mastered the situation like Huberta, is to smother every whimper, grunt, or whine which your mechanism is only too ready to emit. It's heroic to be able to pass through a whole day showing good sportsmanship. And those who have mastered the art of learning to say "Oh, I'm fine, thank you. Just fine!" may prove they are not sissies, but they are definitely indefatigable liars!

The effect of diminishing abilities plays havoc with social, civic and political activity. Sitting at a board meeting is frustrating and useless when you can't hear a word that is being said. And today it appears fashionable to speak in low refined voices which carry an impression that each spoken word is weighted with wisdom.

As for the sort of dinner parties we used to enjoy we simply had to give them up. In by-gone days I loved to put on a pretty evening dress, choose which bracelets and earrings to wear, sparkle with wit through the cocktail hour, and talk intelligently or flirtatiously (depending on the man sitting next to me) through the *filet mignon*, eggplant parmigiana, and Bavarian cream. Getting up from the table, I'd join the ladies as we trouped upstairs to our hostess's bedroom for an elegant cat session. Then downstairs again for half an hour of chitter-chatter with some sleepy, bored husband trying to catch his wife's eye across the room with a pleading look in his own.

Clearly Jim could no longer stand up to this sort of thing, and, although he urged me again and again to go out without him, the time came when I shied away from driving after dark and I was only too glad to stay at home and play dominoes with him. As for our going to the West Indies, that was out of the question, but we did manage to fly as far south as Florida and found the Gasparilla Inn in Boca Grande, a delightful winter sanctuary. Escaping household duties at home was indeed a vacation for me. How I enjoyed our breakfasts in the airy dining room! And how easy was our social life—easy and cheerful in part because Jim's cousin "Dippy" Bartow owned a cottage on the outskirts of the village, and there is nobody more amusing, invigorating and hospitable.

Politically I was still a passionate observer but now distinctly on the sidelines. Mr. Carter was shoved offstage and a Hollywood actor stepped up before the footlights to play the stunning part of "The Great Communicator." What was not in the script was Ronald Reagan's becoming the target of a love-lorn youth with a pistol in his hand—a dramatic episode which Mr. Reagan handled with spontaneous courage and good sportsmanship, giving us a glimpse of the real man beneath the cosmetics. And his second bid for the presidency was so overwhelmingly successful that Republicans couldn't help feeling a bit smug. But Reagan's habit of walking away with a smile over his shoulder and a friendly wave of the hand began to raise questions about whether "The Great Communicator" was, after all, the right man for the job.

Nor was the political picture in Philadelphia cheerful, especially for a life-long Democrat. I was no longer active in local campaigns, other than contributing my bit financially, preferring to leave the strategy sessions and banquets in the hands of the younger people. But after one of our relaxing vacations in Boca Grande I came home refreshed enough to think that I ought to "get into something," not necessarily political but something close by, within reach as it were.

As usual we came home as winter was dwindling away, and spring in fits and starts was bringing out the forsythia, bluebells, and azalea bushes burning bright along our shaded avenues. Spring in the Wissahickon has a special place in the hearts of all of us who live in Chestnut Hill. Since flowers and gardens and springtime always bring to my mind Aunt Carry Sinkler's garden at the Highlands in Fort Washington, I wondered how things were going out there. After her death my cousin Emily and her husband Nick Roosevelt had bought the estate and arranged on their deaths to turn it over to the state "for the benefit of the Commonwealth of Pennsylvania." Unfortunately the commonwealth permitted both house and garden to deteriorate. The beautiful boxwood maze withered, wisteria engulfed the crenelated wall, thieves stole the statuary and broke into the green house, and the garden beds were lost in a tangle of weeds.

In 1973 Frederick Peck, a member of the American Society of Landscape Architecture and a long time resident of Chestnut Hill, wrote a history of the gardens, describing the plans, the boxwood maze, the tool house and the crenelated wall which sheltered the entire garden from the north winds. A turret house at the far end of the wall had only two rooms, one above the other, joined by a tiny circular stairway. It was once the gardener's cottage, and in the Roosevelt règime was turned into a retreat. Emily offered it to me on occasions when I wanted to "get-away-from-it-all." Eventually they added several rooms outside the garden wall and it is now known as "The Pink Palace." In my day the turret was over-run with wistaria wandering across from the wall. Henry McCarter, the artist, captured in a delicate pastel of soft pinks and pale greens the enchanting spirit of what Fred Peck called "the careless unstudied sweetness of the Highlands garden." Long ago Emily gave me the McCarter pastel which now hangs in Jim's room at our Chestnut Hill apartment.

In 1975 neighbors of the Highlands, led by Catherine Moulton, formed the Highlands Historical Society; their objective was to save the estate from complete deterioration. I was invited to join the board and accepted, glad to do what I could to help. It seemed like a way of saying "thank you" to Aunt Carrie and Emily and Nick for the many years of hospitality to me and my friends. During the past years it has been heartening to watch the enthusiasm with which the society members have tackled the stupendous task of restoration. The rejuvenation of the garden was my special interest and it was good news when we won a grant from the Pennsylvania Horticultural Society which enabled us to hire George Patten, a landscape gardener, to work out a restoration plan. After this was finished, several local garden clubs began to work miracles in clearing up and re-planting the garden section by section. I suppose it will never look as I remember it, and now even though the crenelated wall is stripped of the careless tangle of wistaria and the fresh paint on "The Pink Palace" is a little too pink for my taste, those of us who have loved the place are deeply grateful for the work that is being done to preserve it.

Although I did not know it, my concern for the Highlands played a large part in leading me into a new experience—a widening of my interest in historical matters. History in my school days was a dull subject under a wretched teacher, a series of battles lost or won, and lists of generals, admirals, queens and kings. I also remember an examination on British royalty and their dates which turned out to be a fraud—fraud on my part. First I learned by heart that famous rhyme which starts out "First William the Norman, then William his son, Henry, Stephen and Henry, then Richard and John." The rhyme continues all the way up to Queen Victoria. Second, I learned the dates by heart, starting out with "1066 to 1087; 1087 to 1100; 1100 to 1135; 1135 to 1154 . . . "

Third, I made a column of names and placed the appropriate dates beside them. To this day I have no idea which dates belong to which names, but I passed the exam with the mark of 100! I have learned since then that there are more enlightened history teachers, a discovery I was to make indirectly through our own Chestnut Hill Historical Society.

There is a similarity in the compelling forces that gave the Highlands and Chestnut Hill their historical societies. Both began with an accent on architecture. The Highlands' challenge was the restoration of an 18th century Georgian mansion and garden on a three hundred acre estate. Chestnut Hill's Society began by calling themselves "The Committee for the Preservation of Houses and Buildings in Chestnut Hill." In 1967 the name was changed to the "Chestnut Hill Historical Society" and attracted many of us old-timers as well as a large number of young "outsiders" who had moved into our community—people of the same "baby boom" generation as my stepchildren, imbued with a similar sense of mission and public spirit. In the following years several of our unique buildings and houses were restored, and in 1985 Chestnut Hill was named an historical district and placed on the National Register of Historic Places in Washington for our "historical architectural significance."

Privately I was a little surprised at the awakening of my interest in history, and after becoming a member of the Society wondered what I could contribute to their programs. The only thing I could consider the least bit historical in my experience was the leading part that Chestnut Hill and the Philadelphia Cricket Club played in the establishment of women's field hockey in the U.S.A. So one day I carried my collection of field hockey activities dating back to 1915 around the corner to Bob and Nancy Hubby's house on Seminole Avenue. Bob was president of the Society at that time, but it was Nancy Hubby and Shirley Hanson, both active members, who looked over my clippings and photographs. I pointed out that Philadelphia had been the center of field hockey since the game's first introduction to the country in 1904 through Miss Constance Applebee, the sports director at Bryn Mawr College. My punch line was that nine out of fifteen players on the All-American team sent over to England in 1920 had come from Chestnut Hill.

The result of that convivial meeting was a field hockey evening at the Water Tower auditorium. The CHHS sent out invitations that read "Bully for Hockey! An Illustrated Presentation with an All-Star Team of Commentators!" We rounded up a few old-time stars to tell us their favorite field hockey stories and, despite the fact that they had not run up and down a hockey field for fifty years, they were all on hand that night—Virginia Carpenter Biddle, Ella Read Brewster, Lily Cheston Meyers, Sue Goodman Zimmerman and Hazel Coffin Brown. After listening to amusing recollections Ella and I, garbed in old-fashioned tunics, bent over a ball with hockey-sticks in hand taking the stance of a "bully," the opening maneuvre of the game. When Betty Shellenberger, acting as referee, blew the whistle, we hit each other's stick together three times and each scrambled to control the ball. Ella was too quick for me and, with a lightening quick shove, sent the ball back stage.

This little peep into the not-so-distant past had nothing to do with the preservation of historical houses, but it did show that the scope of the society's interests were varied. And when *The Chestnut Hill Local* announced in the fall of 1985 that our historical society was planning a social history of Chestnut Hill, I was intrigued. The plan was to interview older residents and put their reminiscences into book form. This task was undertaken by Dr. David R. Contosta, professor of history and director of American studies at Chestnut Hill College, and author of several books. Although in the throes of completing a history of the United States in the 20th century, he managed to interview over eighty long-time residents and assembled a small library of cassettes bursting with memorable tales about life in our "greene countrie towne." The people interviewed ranged from the late fifties to the mid-nineties and included men and women from all walks of life: gardeners, shop-keepers, grocers, judges, teachers, chauffeurs, *grande dames* and parlour maids.

It was all great fun! Suddenly we old folk were enormously important! The older you were the more important you were! Indeed, what octogenarian does not welcome anyone who will really listen to her? Friends and family soon weary of your oft-repeated tales of "I remember when . . . " But David made listening an art, occasionally tucking in a relevant question to put you back on the track again should you wander too far into what Shippen Lewis used to describe as "ultimate recall." It was a thorough performance and after it was over I felt the way Stanley Woodward did when he said at the end of his interview, "I'm considerably tired of myself."

At one point in my interview David asked a question about my childhood, and I replied with a sigh, "Oh, do we have to go back *that* far? I wrote all that up for *The Local* a few years ago when I was toying with the idea of tackling an autobiography of some sort. Couldn't I give you xeroxed copies of all that?"

He said yes and, busy though he was, took the time to read what I had written. In the meantime, I read his book, *Henry Adams and the American Experiment*, much impressed by the first chapter called "the

165

Making of an Adams." Here was brilliant proof of the new-to-me method of teaching history, and it reminded me of a conversation I had had the previous summer in Maine with Grace Hollander. She had been a history teacher before her marriage and told me that for a long time she had taught history the same way, focusing on a personality and the times in which he lived.

After reading my *Local* articles, David encouraged me to go ahead with what he called an "auto-history."

"Auto-*history*?" I exclaimed. "How could anything I have to say be of the slightest value to an historian?"

"Because you are in a unique position to recapture a lost and enchanted world. Your book could be charming and enjoyable and at the same time valuable to historians," he replied.

I couldn't help thinking about it. I was beginning to catch on to what he was talking about and re-read that first chapter in his *Henry Adams*. The best part was the sudden realization that I wasn't "burnt out" after all! Maybe I could really do it. Perhaps this was the answer to a question I had often asked myself: "Why have I kept all those old diaries, engagement calendars and notebooks filled with philosophical and poetical quotations tucked away in boxes since World War I?" I remember thinking at the time as a phrase or thought interested me that it might come in handy when I got around to writing all those best-selling novels of my dreams. An "auto-history" was not a novel but might it be the answer to these old ambitions?

There were more questions. What would be the theme of such a book? A whole book about myself would be far more confining than letting myself go in a satirical piece like *Device and Desire*. You can tell the truth, the whole truth and nothing but the truth in fiction but not in autobiography. Imagine brazenly putting into print all the times you'd lost your temper, deliberately told a "white lie" and disgracefully did "those things you ought not to have done"—and the reverse!

I began to find answers in a book called *Philadelphia: Patricians and Philistines*, by John Lukacs. A well-known historian and philosopher of history, Lukacs had painted full-length portraits of six Philadelphians, each a powerful example of how to teach history by focusing on an individual. Opposite the title page was a list of other books by the same author, and I pounced on his *Historical Consciousness* or *The Remembered Past*—words that seemed to sum up my own state of mind perfectly. I went to the telephone, called up Hayes Hibberd at Sessler's Bookstore and ordered a copy.

This did the trick. The book is impossible to read from cover to cover.

It is a storehouse of thought that truly boggles the mind! It has to be tapped with care, like an electric power plant which can charge your battery with only so much energy at a time. In it I found more exciting phrases to write down in notebooks for future use. Future use? Did I expect to live forever? At any rate I became intoxicated with the phrase "remembered past." It opened up long avenues of thought while recharging my batteries with a heavy dose of self-confidence. Burnt out? Ridiculous!

Of course I would tackle an "auto-history!" I simply could not pass up this unexpected challenge to set out on another intriguing expedition—not to an island in the West Indies nor to a foreign country, nor even to the far side of the moon, but into time and timelessness! And what about the theme? It was all quite clear now: The book would record ninety years in the life of an adventurous Philadelphian destined to live out her days in twentieth-century America.

So wish me luck! For I'm off on a voyage from 1988 to 1898 and back again. When I swing around full circle the end and the beginning will be one, and perhaps that "lost and enchanting world" will not be lost entirely now that it has been recorded in the remembered past.

Epilogue

NOVEMBER WOODS ARE bare and still. I am sitting near my window looking out at "The View from Eleven Ten" and remembering the brilliant mass of October's flaming colors—scarlet, russet, gold and evergreen, great billowing masses of color softened by the autumn haze.

I am fully alive while writing. I love using a sharp pencil the way a painter loves to apply his brush on canvas. I like to see the words spiraling across the paper. I like to rub out the wrong ones while thumbing through the pages of Roget's *Thesaurus* in search of the right ones. It's a constant treasure hunt, and I think of how the French writer Julian Gracq described it when he said he had written all his years "to settle a score with expression itself; that is, to give form, stability and precision to things that are vague in the mind."

Now that the circle of my expedition into time and timelessness is complete, I feel that despite the energy, care and determination expended, vast areas of emotion and experience remain untouched. The poet's lot is more satisfying. A poem can stand alone, a perfect thing in what it undertakes to say.

Hence this epilogue: a kind of inescapable soliloquy. Elbows on desk, chin in hands, it is easy to close my eyes and drift into a sort of reverie. Pictures, one after the other, begin to race across my private TV screen. Out of context, vivid, painful, humorous, beautiful and saddening, they chase each other faster than a three-second political campaign advertisement . . . *Scene*: Dinner-party at the Byam Stevens' house in Maryland; my cousin Clare, better known as "Chattie" sits at head of table; someone mentions F.D.R. and, knowing her husband's feelings about him as well as mine, she takes charge and clips disaster in the bud by saying firmly, "There will be no political talk at this table to-night!" . . . Discovery of a copy of *The Petrified Gesture* in the library aboard the Cunard liner *Queen Mary*; Mother sitting under a tree near the hotel at Fishers' Island

169

reading *The House of the Wolf* to Eleanor and me when I was eight years old; a certain New Year's Day when all of Chestnut Hill turned out to go skating on the black ice of the Wissahickon Creek near Valley Green; Shippen's keen delight in our springtime canoe trips shooting the rapids on the upper Delaware; the delicious sponge cake Molly Duffy used to make at our house on Hartwell Avenue; the desolation I felt when I watched my second lieutenant of the 311th Field Artillery climb up the steps of a train at St. Martin's Station which took him away to the western front; a glorious morning walk with Anne Fishburne along the old rice embankment at Mulberry Hall, South Carolina, when the carolling of songbirds outsang the grunts and cries of rail birds, bitterns and ibises in the swamp; Dora and me, swimming across the harbor at Bermuda from Glencoe to the Princess hotel—beautiful, loveable step-daughter who died of cancer at the age of forty-three; my first opera at the Philadelphia Opera House with Tito Ruffo singing in Cavalleria Rusticana; winning fourteen dollars on my way back home on the Southern Pacific Railroad from the H.F. Bar Ranch in Wyoming; gambling at "21" with strangers; conversing with Chief Justice Hughes at a very grand reception—the only time I have ever been in The White House; The chocolate *mousse* in Paris which Jim still wishes he had ordered instead of *fraises de bois*; breaking a Pinelands Camp record on field day by running fifty yards in six and a half seconds; Audrey Saylor's words that spoke for all of us when she said, leaving Charlie Woodward's eightieth birthday party at Krisheim, "I've just been talking to four hundred of my most intimate friends;" The delicious feeling of buoyancy and freedom when pushing off in my kayak from our float at Pretty Marsh; Father teaching us hymns at 322 Moreland Avenue, sitting in the arbor and sending us to the snowball bush for the first line, to the iron gate for the second, to the lilacs for the third and back to him for the fourth . . .

The split-second flashes could go on and on, and with an effort I break through the barrier of timelessness and find myself in the present moment writing this and thinking "1898!" Almost a century away and I am face to face with ninety years behind me! Not yet however, is my "pitcher broken at the fountain;"* desire fail, and life too high a mountain for me to climb. Time has now become a sacred thing, each fresh new morning giving me a chance for gratitude, because of having lived it all.

*Ecclesiastes xii:6.